Laying Down the Law

Laying Down
the Law

KEITH AUGUSTUS BURTON

REVIEW AND HERALD® PUBLISHING ASSOCIATION
Since 1861 | www.reviewandherald.com

Published by Review and Herald® Publishing Association, Hagerstown, MD 21741-1119

Review and Herald® titles may be purchased in bulk for educational, business, fund-raising, or sales promotional use. For information, e-mail SpecialMarkets@reviewandherald.com.

The Review and Herald® Publishing Association publishes biblically based materials for spiritual, physical, and mental growth and Christian discipleship.

The author assumes full responsibility for the accuracy of all facts and quotations as cited in this book.

Unless otherwise indicated, Bible texts in this book are from the New Revised Standard Version of the Bible, copyright © 1989 by the Division of Christian Education of the National Council of the Churches of Christ in the U.S.A. Used by permission.

Texts credited to NIV are from the *Holy Bible, New International Version.* Copyright © 1973, 1978, 1984, 2011 by Biblica, Inc. Used by permission. All rights reserved worldwide.

Texts credited to NKJV are from the New King James Version. Copyright © 1979, 1980, 1982 by Thomas Nelson, Inc. Used by permission. All rights reserved.

This book was
Edited by Gerald Wheeler
Copyedited by Delma Miller
Cover Design by Emily Ford/Review and Herald® Design Center
Cover Illlustration by Lars Justinen
Interior Design by Derek Knecht/Review and Herald® Design Center
Typeset: Minion Pro 11/13

PRINTED IN U.S.A.

17 16 15 14 13   5 4 3 2 1

Library of Congress Cataloging-in-Publication Data

Burton, Keith Augustus.
  Laying down the law / Keith Burton.
    pages cm
  ISBN 978-0-8280-2746-5
  1. Law and gospel. I. Title.
  BT79.B87 2013
  241'.2--dc23

                        2013014176

ISBN 978-0-8280-2746-5

Dedication

To my parents, Nehemiah Augustus Burton and Cynthia Yvonne Morgan-Burton, who taught me to love God's law through their countless acts of grace.

Contents

Preface

After returning from an exhausting overseas ministry trip, I decided to catch up on work in the church office. The day was busier than I had anticipated, and after a few hours jet lag attacked my sobriety. My body was telling me to go home and get some needed rest, but it was almost time for prayer meeting and I was on the pastoral staff. After my free-falling neck jerked me into consciousness for the umpteenth time, I decided that prayer meeting would not be seeing my face that evening. Just so I wouldn't have to explain my planned absence to anyone, I decided to wait until the prayer meeting attendees were comfortably settled inside the building before I made my exit.

I felt as guilty as a teenager sneaking out of their parents' house as I crept into my car and stealthily slipped out of the parking lot. After all, the pastor for administration was not supposed to skip prayer meeting, was he? My body's yearning for rest affected my attentiveness, and I was totally oblivious to the fact that I was driving 10 miles per hour above the speed limit on a road known for its police presence. But the sudden appearance of blue-and-white strobe lights, rhythmically bouncing from my rearview mirror, awakened me from my oblivion. Only then did I realize that the ringing sound in my ear was not caused by temporary tinnitus, but came from the amplified sirens on the officer's car.

Still focused on sleep, I didn't even try to protest the ticket. Although I never left the church office with the intention of breaking the law, when I first noticed the police car behind me I immediately looked at my speedometer and knew that I was in violation. Why protest when I had seen the evidence of my infraction? Perhaps my unwillingness to appeal to any crumb of mercy that may have resided in the officer's heart also resulted from the guilt of skipping out on prayer meeting. If I had taken my tired self to prayer meeting that evening, I thought to myself, *I would have escaped this ticket.*

As I reflect on the experience, I find myself questioning my reasoning process. It's almost as if I concluded that God had punished me with a speeding ticket for neglecting to attend prayer meeting. However, who's to say that I wouldn't have gotten one if I *had* gone to the service and then ventured home with an even more intense fatigue? Further, when did it become a sin for a jet-lagged person to miss a church service? Is God really waiting in a hard-to-spot location to issue citations to speeding sinners? If God were the ticketing officer, would He have convicted me if He knew that I was unaware that I was breaking the law?

I have written this book to explore what the Bible has to say about God's reaction to people who have violated His law. In other words, it's about God's response to all of us. After all, every one of us has sinned. Each chapter will present the law through the perspective of Christ the blessed Son who entered our reality to give us a more perfect picture of His Father. It will not take long for the reader to see that God's righteous law is a partner with grace in the work of salvation. Those who choose to enter into a covenant relationship with Christ will voluntarily submit their selfish desires to His law of love as they incorporate the principles of God's eternal kingdom into their earthly lives.

CHAPTER 1

Laws in Christ's Day

In the summer of 1998 I received an invitation to teach a graduate course at Solusi University in Fig Tree, Zimbabwe. The students in the program were pastors and conference administrators from a number of African countries. It was my first time on the continent from which my ancestors hailed, and I was eager to *learn* all I could about the different cultures represented in the cohort I was contracted to teach. I quickly learned the regional greeting for Matabeleland, which became an effective icebreaker and bridge to learning other greetings. For instance, after practicing my newly acquired vocabulary, one Zimbabwean informed me that he was Shona, so instead of saying "sali bonani" when I saw him (the traditional Ndebele greeting), I would say "makidini."

Another student who hailed from Botswana not only trained me to greet him with "dumela," but invited me to accompany him on a road trip to Gaborone one weekend. While we traveled through the dusty Kalahari Desert, he informed me of the purpose of his visit. My young unmarried student was excited that his single status would soon change. However, before he could enjoy marital bliss, he had to address some customary details—particularly the negotiation of a dowry with his future in-laws.

Our weekend visit coincided with a nationwide cultural camp meeting at which youth from around the country assembled to camp, fellowship, and be spiritually fed in the open air. A high point of the weekend was former Botswana president Quett Ketumile Joni Masire sitting around the campfire and in his own fatherly way sharing the details of African marriage traditions with a new generation slowly being captivated by Western norms. Sitting intently, I soaked in the details about the proper protocol and the role that the "uncles" played in the negotiations. Also I learned that Tswana culture negotiated the bride-price in heads of cattle.

My host wasn't present during the presentation—coincidentally, he was with his family waiting to receive the negotiation report from his uncle. I could not wait until I saw him that afternoon so that I could impress him with my newfound knowledge. My suggestion that since his future father-in-law was a strict vegan, he could probably save a lot of money by negotiating for his bride in heads of cabbage rather than cattle left us both laughing.

Then my mind wandered to my own betrothal experience 11 years before. While Western culture has no prescribed process that carries the force of law, fragments of nonbinding traditions remind us of a time that people expected certain protocols before a marriage. Even now I clearly remember the day that two families who had known each other for less than four days assembled in the basement of James Melancon's home to celebrate my engagement to my future wife. I approached my father-in-law and requested permission to propose to his daughter. Once I received the green light, I turned toward my intended, got down on one knee, and asked if she would be my wife. Already knowing what the answer would be, I swiftly moved to the next act, in which I presented her with a shiny gold-plated watch that I took pleasure in securing on her extended wrist.

Things were different in Africa. I had acted out my proposal with chivalrous pretense, but it was not really necessary. As far as American society was concerned, we could have just gone to a courthouse and entered into a marriage without any required rituals. Although our parents would have been disappointed, we would not have been violating any societal or cultural customs or laws. However, in many African cultures the prenuptial activities are not scenes in an optional play. They are mandatory rules that every member of the community must follow. Although most African societies had been subject to various expressions of European law as a result of colonial rule, they still consider the age-old customs that had brought stability to their ancestors as binding on contemporary generations.

Roman Law

The legal layers that govern the lives of many traditional Africans provide us insight into the numerous cultures and societies that comprised the New Testament world. It was a world populated by people groups who had to learn to balance their cultural laws with those of the imperial power that had colonized them. Indeed, Rome was a society that valued the rule of law and demanded that all under its jurisdiction submit to its authoritative code.

Historians can trace the Roman legal system to the fifth century B.C. and the establishment of the Twelve Tables. Unfortunately, while the traditions surrounding the development of the Twelve Tables have survived, the tables themselves have vanished, and only fragments of their content still exist. Notwithstanding, Roman jurists continued to develop legislation, and by the time of Jesus' birth the empire had a fully developed system of law that governed all areas of life.

As we investigate the New Testament, we see several places that clearly demonstrate the role of Roman law in the lives of the biblical characters, even though a number of them were Jews living in lands outside of Italy. For instance, in Luke 2:1, 2 we learn that the Caesar named Augustus decreed a comprehensive census for all subjects in the Roman Empire. Apparently the law stipulated that the head of the family had to fulfill the terms of the census in his town of origin. Although Jesus' earthly parents were Jews living in Nazareth at the time and were not Roman citizens, they had to participate even if it meant that they had to make an inconvenient trip to Joseph's hometown of Bethlehem while Mary was late into her third term of pregnancy.

Another New Testament text further illustrates how Roman law affected the liberties of certain segments of the populace. In His sermon on the mount, as Jesus discussed the traits of heavenly kingdom citizens, He referred to a law that allowed soldiers to demand services for them even if it went against a person's will (Matt. 5:41).[1] We see the principle behind the law in a memorable incident that occurred during Jesus' final trek down the Via Dolorosa when the Roman soldiers ordered Simon from the North African province of Cyrene to carry their prisoner's cross to the place of execution (Matt. 27:32).

Roman law worked best for those privileged with citizenship. People so cherished the benefits of citizenship that they willingly paid great sums of money for the status (cf. Acts 22:28). In Roman society the vast majority of people were noncitizens, with many classified as slaves. Above slaves were the *freedmen*—those fortunate enough to be emancipated by a benevolent master or who had earned enough to purchase their freedom. The children of freedmen were the *freeborn*, and thus had the right to buy citizenship. Once you became a citizen, your offspring automatically had the status.

The apostle Paul happened to be among the privileged few who held Roman citizenship. During a conversation with a Roman legionnaire, he carefully pointed out that his citizenship was a result of birth and not purchase (verse 28). Although a proud Jew, Paul did not shy from taking full advantage of the status acquired at birth. He may not have liked the fact that his people were under foreign occupation, but he had sense enough to take full advantage of the protections provided him by the law. Fully aware of his rights, he reminded the authorities after they imprisoned and beat him without a trial that they had broken the law, and audaciously demanded a personal apology from those responsible (Acts 16:35-40).

The same fear that filled those who had not followed due process before imprisoning Paul was felt by the Roman tribune, whose plans to scourge the apostle he thwarted by his appeal for his rights (Acts 22:29; cf. verses 22-28). The frightened tribune went the extra mile to protect Paul from the Jewish authorities who wanted him dead. After the discovery that an assassination team had vowed to take Paul's life by any means necessary, the same tribune arranged for the apostle's safe passage to Caesarea, where the soldiers placed him in the custody of the Roman governor, Felix.

The Jewish prosecutors in Caesarea attempted to have him extradited to Jerusalem, where they felt they would have a better chance of securing the death penalty—whether through legal or mercenary means. They would have been successful had Paul not taken advantage of the ultimate right a Roman citizen had in his quest for justice: he petitioned the transfer of his case to Caesar (Acts 25:1-12). So precious a right was such a request that once made it could not be nullified. After hearing Paul's defense, King Agrippa lamented to Festus, "This man could have been set free if he had not appealed to the emperor" (Acts 26:32).

While Paul took full advantage of his citizenship status, at times he willingly confronted Roman law for the sake of the gospel. While in Philippi, Macedonia, Paul and his companions ministered to a female entrepreneur named Lydia. Already familiar with the Jewish understanding of God, Lydia accepted the message of Christ and invited the apostle to minister to her household, which resulted in more people joining God's kingdom. On the surface it seems a harmless conversion story. However, assuming that Lydia and those in her household were Roman citizens, it was a serious offense. The grave nature of Paul's actions does not manifest itself until the events that took place after he had exorcised a demon-possessed slave girl in Philippi. When her owner pressed charges against him, they specifically accused him of "advocating customs that are not lawful for . . . Romans to adopt or observe" (Acts 16:21). It almost got Paul lynched. Although beaten and imprisoned, he escaped further penalties only by asserting his citizenship rights (verses 20-24).

The fact that Paul was a Roman citizen who also adhered to the Jewish faith indicates that it was not against the law for Romans to practice Judaism. However, the incident in Philippi also implies that the law forbade overt attempts to convert citizens. Notwithstanding, Paul's bifurcated status meant that he was subject to two tiers of political laws. For instance, when he founded the church in Corinth, the local Jewish leaders had him arrested and brought before the local proconsul, Gallio. The charge was similar to the one brought against him by Roman citizens in Philippi when they accused him of "persuading people to worship God in ways that are contrary to the law" (Acts 18:13). Whereas attempts to proselytize Romans constituted a crime, in this particular case Gallio interpreted Roman law another way and concluded, "If it were a matter of crime or serious villainy, I would be justified in accepting the complaint of you Jews; but since it is a matter of questions about words and names and your own law, see to it yourselves; I do not wish to be a judge of these matters" (verses 14, 15). We see the rights of the Jews to negotiate issues pertaining to their own religion demonstrated by the fact that Gallio turned a blind eye to the mob beating of Sosthenes, a synagogue official who had apparently accepted Jesus as Messiah (verse 17).

Not only did Roman law permit Jews under imperial jurisdiction to adjudicate religious or civil cases, but at times the Jewish authorities would involve themselves in capital cases. We clearly view this in Jesus' trial when the impromptu court headed by Caiaphas imposed the death penalty on Him. After the sentencing, they transferred Him to the offices of Pontius Pilate, the Roman procurator. Sensing trouble, Pilate immediately appealed to the same legal clause that Gallio used in Corinth as he attempted to dismiss Jesus' inquisitors with the order "Take him yourselves and judge him according to your law" (John 18:31). However, knowing that they had already reached their decision and the limits the law placed on them when it came to implementing punishment, they protested, "We are not permitted to put anyone to death" (verse 31).

We encounter still other details about Roman law in the events that follow. Apparently, before Pilate could administer the death sentence, he had to cross-examine the accused (verses 33-37). It soon became evident to him that Jesus was an innocent man, and he sought to have Him acquitted on the basis of a negotiated Jewish-Roman law that allowed for the pardon of a prisoner during Passover, but the incensed mob would not have it (verses 38-40). Pilate's symbolic washing of the hands was not enough to loosen the ties that compelled him to carry through the death sentence, but he needed a legitimate reason to execute a man he believed to be innocent. The inscription placed on Jesus' cross says it all: "Jesus of Nazareth, the King of the Jews." From the perspective of Roman law, Jesus was a potential insurrectionist who challenged the very throne of the emperor (cf. John 19:8-22).

Mosaic Civil Law

Although the Jewish authorities had limited powers when it came to meting out the penalty for capital cases, they had broad authority in matters pertaining to everyday life in Jewish society. The Romans were skilled at accommodating the culture of those whom they conquered, and in the same spirit in which they permitted Greek (rather than Latin) to serve as the lingua franca of the empire, they allowed the Jews to maintain their own laws. Judging from the mob assault on Sosthenes in Corinth, such authority extended to any part of the empire containing an established Jewish community.[2] Nonetheless, the center of Jewish law would have been in Jerusalem.

While we have little historical evidence for how the Jews administered their laws at this time, it has been customary to follow a second-century rabbinic tradition suggesting that ultimate legal authority rested in a judicial body known by the common Greek term *Sanhedrin*.[3] Also called in Hebrew the *bêt dîn* (Great Court), the Sanhedrin reportedly consisted of 71 distinguished members of Jewish society headed by the high priest. Based on evidence from the extensive Jewish commentary on Scripture known as the Mishnah, the Sanhedrin had a threefold role: "It made final decisions in legal disputes, judged the fitness of priests to serve in the temple, and decided on additions to the temple."[4]

Jewish societal law had its basis in the biblical laws of Moses that had been in place for more than seven centuries before the Romans' Twelve Tables. So central were they to Israel that even though a major part of its content is historical drama, the section of the Bible in which they appear is simply called *Torah*, a Hebrew term for law. Whereas many of the laws given to Moses related to the sanctuary and sacrificial system that formed the core of Israelite life, a number of them were distinct civil laws that governed societal behavior. As the original constitution of a civilization that even the Romans would have called "ancient," the Mosaic code was only slightly subordinated to Roman law in first-century Palestine. While the will of the emperor was paramount, the Roman authorities knew that a semblance of freedom for their newly acquired vassals would lessen the chances of insurrection.

One of the freedoms that the otherwise subjugated Jewish government enjoyed was the right to levy taxes. Not only did Jewish men still have to satisfy their tax obligations to the empire, but they also had to pay a half-shekel Temple tax each March. The Torah spells out the terms of the tax:

"And the Lord spoke unto Moses, saying: 'When thou takest the sum of the children of Israel, according to their number, then shall they give every man a ransom for his soul unto the Lord, when thou numberest them; that there be no plague among them, when thou numberest them. This they shall give, every one that passeth among them that are numbered, half a shekel after the shekel of the sanctuary—the shekel is twenty gerahs—half a shekel for an offering to the Lord. Every one that passeth among them that are numbered, from twenty years old and upward, shall give the offering of the Lord. The rich shall not give more, and the poor shall not give less, than the half shekel, when they give the offering of the Lord, to make atonement for your souls'" (Ex. 30:11-15).

Although permanent temples constructed by Solomon, Zerubbabel, and Herod had since replaced the portable sanctuary that initially benefited from the law, the principle behind it was relevant as long as the Jews maintained a sacred place for worship and sacrifice. Revenue agents who had the authority to collect taxes continued to enforce the law. Apparently some questioned whether Jesus was compliant with the law and interrogated Peter about it. Although the disciple answered in the affirmative, it does not appear as if Jesus necessarily agreed with the compulsory nature of the law, but paid the taxes nonetheless (Matt. 17:24-27).

Mosaic law also served as the foundation for laws relating to marriage. When the Pharisees approached Jesus with a question about acceptable grounds for divorce, He initially directed them to the relevant section of the Torah that stipulated the terms of divorce and remarriage (cf. Matt. 19:7; Deut. 24:1-4).[5] Jesus also tussled with the Sadducees over a Mosaic law that detailed what should happen if a man dies before his wife has had a chance to bear him a son:

"When brothers reside together, and one of them dies and has no son, the wife of the deceased shall not be married outside the family to a stranger. Her husband's brother shall go in to her, taking her in marriage, and performing the duty of a husband's brother to her, and the firstborn whom she bears shall succeed to the name of the deceased brother, so that his name shall not be blotted out of Israel" (Deut. 25:5, 6).

Of course, when the Sadducees referred to the passage, they were really using it as a basis to disprove the resurrection (cf. Matt. 22:23-33). However, the fact that they even raise it proves that this facet of Mosaic law still remained in effect in New Testament times.

Not only did Mosaic law stipulate the steps to follow after the divorce or death of a spouse, it presented the harshest of penalties for those guilty of adultery: "If a man is caught lying with the wife of another man, both of them shall die, the man who lay with the woman as well as the woman" (Deut. 22:22). The customary method of capital punishment in cases of adultery was stoning (cf. verses 21, 24). We see the continued applicability of this law in the New Testament account of the woman caught in the "very act" of adultery (John 8:1-11). The fact that she was found guilty without a trial meant that she was either married or engaged. If she were single, she would have been pressed into marriage with the man (cf. Deut. 22:28, 29). The account also implies that at times ordinary Jewish citizens independently determine that they will ignore the imperial law that restricted the right to implement capital punishment to the Roman government (cf. Acts 6:8-8:1). Because frenzied mobs often carried out such public lynchings, the Roman authorities probably felt it wise not to intervene so as to avert wide-scale rioting from a people who already despised foreign presence in their homeland.

Whether carried out by official or unofficial channels, the law of Moses is clear about the due process that must precede capital punishment: "On the evidence of two or three witnesses the death sentence shall be executed; a person must not be put to death on the evidence of only one witness. The hands of the witnesses shall be the first raised against the person to execute the death penalty, and afterward the hands of all the people" (Deut. 17:6, 7). It is on the basis of this statute that Jesus asks the woman caught in adultery, "Woman, where are they? Has no one condemned you?" (John 8:10). The Sanhedrin manipulated the statute when they conjured two false witnesses to convict Jesus (Matt. 26:59, 60).

Ceremonial Law

The Sanhedrin's religious makeup reflected the fact that Israel had been a *theocracy*. In those territories under quasi-Jewish control clerics were the ones who called the shots. A theocracy considers all activities as religious. For Jews of the first century, the entire law was a means to a spiritual end. If the people were faithful to their legal responsibilities, they would be in right standing with God and thus qualified to receive His forgiveness through Temple sacrifices.

The civil and religious laws are somewhat intertwined in the Torah (first five books of the Bible). Indeed, in all appearances they were presented to the original society as one unified law. However, it is not hard to see that the laws do fall into two distinct categories. As we noticed in the previous section, some laws dealt with civic issues. In this section, we will isolate examples of laws that were purely religious in nature.

Anyone visiting Jerusalem at the time of Jesus would quickly notice the imposing Temple that Herod the Great had enlarged to occupy 1.5 million square feet (144,000 square meters) of Jerusalem real estate![6] Although the foreign Herod probably embarked on the project to beef up his already-remarkable architectural résumé, the Temple was a symbol of pride for his Jewish subjects. An impressive upgrade from earlier structures, the Temple indicated the only location on earth where God dwelled in His shekinah. It was the place where the people of promise received their affirmation of the presence of God as they had their sins erased through real and meaningful ways.

As we learn from the Old Testament, access to the Temple services was not an automatic right for the descendants of Jacob. In order to get close to God's earthly presence, His people had to be ritually clean. Often a person's health or gender-based biological activities determined a person's ritual cleanliness. Consider the following:

1. "When any man has a discharge from his member, his discharge makes him ceremonially unclean" (Lev. 15:2).
2. "If a man has an emission of semen, he shall bathe his whole body in water, and be unclean until the evening" (verse 16).
3. "When a woman has a discharge of blood that is her regular discharge from her body, she shall be in her impurity for seven days, and whoever touches her shall be unclean until the evening" (verse 19).
4. "If a woman has a discharge of blood for many days, not at the time of her impurity, or if she has a discharge beyond the time of her impurity, all the days of the discharge she shall continue in uncleanness; as in the days of her impurity she shall be unclean" (verse 25).

Indeed, it is the latter of these categories that affected the unnamed woman in the Gospels who had been hemorrhaging for 12 years (Luke

8:43-48). According to the law, everything she touched and everyone who came into contact with her would immediately become unclean (see Lev. 15:26, 27). In pushing through the crowd to see Jesus, she realized that she was contaminating scores of people. However, her desperation led her to violate a law that seemingly held her captive. One can only imagine how spiritually depraved she must have felt after being denied access to the only visible place where she could have her burden removed.

In addition to men and women who experienced gender-related discharges, those suffering from a number of skin diseases that came under the category of "leprosy" also found themselves barred from the Temple.[7] The law is clear on the matter:

"When a person has on the skin of his body a swelling or an eruption or a spot, and it turns into a leprous disease on the skin of the body, he shall be brought to Aaron the priest or to one of his sons the priests. The priest shall examine the disease on the skin of his body, and if the hair in the diseased area has turned white and the disease appears to be deeper than the skin of his body, it is a leprous disease; after the priest has examined him he shall pronounce him ceremonially unclean" (Lev. 13:2, 3).

The priest played the role of community health officer. His authority to certify a person's ceremonial cleanliness was not limited only to leprosy, but extended to all other health-related incidents. Knowing the central role of the priest in determining the ceremonial health of an individual, Jesus carefully instructed those whom He healed from leprosy to follow the mandated protocol (cf. Luke 17:11-19). In fact, when He heals the leper after delivering the Sermon on the Mount, He reminds him that he once again has access to the Temple where he will be free to make sacrifices (Matt. 8:1-4).

Whereas leprosy was an external indication of a person's ceremonial uncleanness, the Mosaic law had an interesting section detailing how a person could externally manifest their ceremonial zeal: the Nazirite vow. "When either men or women make a special vow, the vow of a nazirite, to separate themselves to the Lord, they shall separate themselves from wine and strong drink. . . . All the days of their nazirite vow no razor shall come upon their head; until the time is completed for which they separate themselves to the Lord, they shall be holy; they shall let the locks of the head grow long" (Num. 6:2-5).

Although the vow was temporary, those who undertook it would not even break it to attend their parents' funeral, since contact with the dead made one ceremonially unclean (see Num. 6:6, 7). Interestingly, the apostle Paul undertook the vow and even participated in purification rites with four other Christian men whose Nazirite period had ended (cf. Acts 18:18; 21:22-27; Num. 6:13-21). Given the belief that Christ has superseded the Temple, some may wonder why Paul's obvious adherence to a statute of the ceremonial law was fully endorsed—even encouraged—by the top leadership of the fledgling church. However, we must not forget that the church at this point was still in its teething stages and had not yet experienced full separation from its Jewish parent. Further, it is also possible that motivation for mission was the driving force behind their continued cultural conformity (1 Cor. 9:22, 23).

Rabbinic Law

When James encouraged Paul to participate in the Nazirite purification ritual, he did it with the hope that the act would pacify overzealous Jewish leaders who had accused Paul of diluting the doctrines of Judaism (see Acts 21:17ff). What made the situation even more volatile was the fact that the apostle himself had once been one of these extremists, and had done all in his power to quash the fledgling Jesus movement. In his former life Paul had identified with the party of the Pharisees, widely known for strict adherence to the Jewish law. As far as Jesus was concerned, the problem with the Pharisees was not so much that they taught fidelity to the law, but that their actions were often hypocritical and their understanding of the merciful principle behind God's law was warped (see Matt. 23:1ff.).

While the origin of the Pharisees is still a subject of debate, scholars generally believe that they emerged during the period after the Maccabean Revolution had freed the Jews of Palestine from the rule of the Selucid Empire. To all appearances, they were aligned with the teachers of the Mosaic law that later generations respectfully called "rabbis," a term that means "my teacher."[8] According to tradition, the rabbis taught that if all Israel were to keep the law for just one day, the Messiah would make His appearance. As a means to this grand objective, the rabbis felt that it was necessary to build a "hedge" around the law.

The "hedge" consisted of a number of other regulations based on the rabbis' interpretation of the biblical laws of Moses. If the people would keep the lesser laws, they reasoned, they would automatically observe the greater ones by default. The first step to their grand quest involved enumerating all Mosaic laws, which they calculated as 613. Then they thematically categorized the laws. For instance, they isolated 39 regulations on the Sabbath alone. Finally it became the responsibility of the expositors of the law to teach the people how to keep it.

The interpretations of the rabbis are known as *halakhah* (plural = *halakhoth*), which in the Hebrew means "to walk." Eventually the oral edicts got written down and in a very real sense became as authoritative as the very Mosaic law on which they were based. Although a diversity of interpretations existed among the rabbis—ranging from conservative to liberal—people generally believed that they should respect and follow the men's words. Many of the scholarly opinions that circulated in the New Testament world became codified along with later ones about two centuries after the time of Christ. The collection in which they appear, known as the Mishnah, remains an authoritative source for many Jews even today.

We see evidence of rabbinic law in several places in the New Testament. For instance, when the Pharisees and scribes accuse Jesus' disciples of breaking "the tradition of the elders," they point to a custom that mandated the washing of hands before the consumption of food (Matt. 15:1-6). Apparently the teachers of the law who developed the doctrine reasoned that unwashed hands could have touched something defiled or unclean and would consequently defile the food being consumed. In a roundabout way, it would render the person ceremonially unclean.

Other instances of rabbinic law appear in Matthew's account of Jesus' famous denouncement of the hypocrisy of the scribes and Pharisees. The first reflects a time in Jewish history that prohibited speaking the name of God, so people who made oaths had to find a way to swear on something holy without violating the prohibition. We learn from Jesus' words that the teachers of the law taught that "whoever swears by the altar is bound by nothing, but whoever swears by the gift that is on the altar is bound by the oath" (Matt. 23:18). Although the Pharisees may have felt that they were honoring the divine name by uttering an oath in such a manner, Jesus utilizes a rather clever deductive argument to show that swearing by the gift is no different than swearing by God (verses 19-22)!

Jesus' rebuke of the Pharisees' hypocrisy also calls attention to the scrupulous way in which they tithed. The original Mosaic instructions on tithing originated in an agricultural context and probably assumed that people would return tithe on their annual harvests. However, in their attempt to build a hedge around the law, the Pharisees promoted the tithing of garden herbs probably grown only in small quantities to season food (verse 23).

Although Jesus' lecture to the Pharisees is rife with harsh words, His aim was restorative. He wanted them to see that in adding layers to the Mosaic law they had neglected to recognize the true principle behind divine law: "justice and mercy and faith" (verse 23). They had missed the purpose for which God had given the law to Israel in the first place, and had formed a relationship with the law rather than its Giver. It is to these misguided fellows that Jesus laments, "So you also on the outside look righteous to others, but inside you are full of hypocrisy and lawlessness" (verse 28). By emphasizing legalistic adherence to a set of codes that exceeded the biblical witness, the Pharisees and their rabbinic heirs had placed the letter over the spirit.

Covenant Law

In an earlier scene from Matthew's Gospel, Jesus had already established the law upon which God judges the level of human spirituality. An anonymous man approached Him and asked, "Teacher, what good deed must I do to have eternal life?" (Matt. 19:16). Without hesitation, Jesus responds, "If you wish to enter into life, keep the commandments" (verse 17). Given the number of commandments that bombarded the Judean populace, we should not be surprised when Jesus' inquisitor asks, "Which ones?"

Indeed, we have already seen that people of New Testament times were subject to any number of laws. Given the fact that the inquiry dealt with spiritual issues, it is obvious that the question did not even consider the various statutes associated with Roman law. Rather, "Which ones?" sought to identify the basic religious laws that opened the path to eternal rewards. Jesus had the option of pointing to the various rituals from the law of Moses that detailed the path to ceremonial cleanliness. Alternatively, He could have pointed to injunctions in the Mosaic societal code that dealt with issues such as Temple taxation or gender-based dress. He could even have elevated parts of the rabbinic law designed to stop sin before it happened. However, He refers to none of those. Instead, He responds, "You shall not murder; You shall not commit adultery; You shall not steal; You shall not bear false witness; Honor your father and mother; also, You shall love your neighbor as yourself" (verses 18, 19).

In no uncertain terms Jesus points the inquirer to the Ten Commandments. Given his response, it is possible that it was the answer that the man expected. The Jews in the world of the Gospels pretty much accepted that the Ten Commandments comprised the essential core of God's law. Philo, a Jewish philosopher and contemporary of Jesus, wrote an entire book on the central place the Ten Commandments had among all biblical law. We later learn from the Mishnah that the rabbis believed that daily recital of the Ten Commandments was the equivalent of reciting the entire law (*Tamid* 5:1). Further, when other New Testament authors provide the essential content of God's obligatory law, they cite the Ten Commandments (see Rom. 13:8-10; James 2:8-12).

Leslie Hoppe provides the reason for the elevated role of the Ten Commandments in Scripture: "The biblical tradition presents the commandments as the basis upon which Israel's continuing relationship with God becomes possible. God's deliverance of Israel from slavery in Egypt established that relationship. The Ten Commandments provide Israel with the moral framework for maintaining it. The metaphor that the Bible uses to express this relationship is covenant. While the metaphor comes from the sphere of international law, it is wrong to understand the commandments merely as a summary of Israel's legal obligations toward God. . . . Israel's obedience to the commandments was not a matter of submission to the divine will as much as it was a response of love."[9]

In citing the Ten Commandments, Jesus reminds the anonymous man about the terms of the covenant that God had made with his ancestors. However, notice that Jesus doesn't just end with the quotation of Scripture, because He knows that God's promise of eternal life is for those who desire an eternal *relationship* with Him. A divine principle binds the commandments together, hence Jesus' reference to the overarching commandment that summarizes the second table of the Decalogue: "You shall love your neighbor as yourself." Still fixated on conformity to external rules, the young man answers, "I have kept all these; what do I still lack?" (Matt. 19:20).

It is not clear whether he responded out of boastful confidence or if the inquirer had a genuine sense of emptiness even after he had tried his best to conform himself to divine acceptance. Whatever his motive, Christ responded by appealing to his deepest spiritual sensibilities. "If you wish to be perfect, go, sell your possessions, and give the money to the poor, and you will have treasure in heaven; then come, follow me" (verse 21). The young man had to know that God did not intend obedience to His law to be a laborious checklist that leaves an empty feeling in the heart of the doer. The keeping of commandments in a spiritual context has meaning only when a person is filled and inspired by the same love that resides in the realm of the God who delivers politically, physically, and spiritually. Those in a true covenant relationship with God will not have to ask what they must do to inherit eternal life, because the Spirit of God would already be controlling their actions.

Conclusion

As we have seen, it was possible for people living in the New Testament world to find themselves subject to any number of laws. Depending on where they lived, they could have been required to observe Roman imperial law, Mosaic civic and ceremonial law, or rabbinic law. A violation of any of the legal codes would have led to various degrees of penalties. In a very real sense, all the laws were somewhat restrictive and may even have stirred fear in the hearts of those compelled to live under them.

If they were the only laws one encountered in the Bible, it would not be wrong to assign a negative connotation on all law. However, the Bible also features a law that is above every other, because it forms the basis of the covenant that God has with His people. It was the Ten Commandment law that is beyond human enforcement. Since it does not confuse external conformity with true transformation of character, it is not subject to human enforcement, because God alone has the power to place His loving Spirit in the willing hearts of women and men who desire an eternal relationship with Him.

On the weekend that I drove with my student from Fig Tree, Zimbabwe, to Gaborone, Botswana, another person rode with us in the car. He was one of the scheduled speakers for the weekend meeting and had begun his trip on a bus from Harare. After our time of ministry and socializing that weekend, I would never have dreamed that five years later I would have bumped into him in a church where I served in Alabama. Interestingly, I learned that one of his purposes for relocating to the United States was to solidify a relationship with a beautiful foreign student from Zimbabwe who would soon become his wife.

Since they were both in America, I figured that it would not be too difficult for them to arrange for a marriage. However, I was soon to learn that although they were separated from their homeland by thousands of miles, they still had to uphold their traditional laws of marriage. The uncles still had to negotiate the dowry, and he had to observe other protocols. I still remember sharing the pain in my friend's spirit when he had to pay a hefty fine to his in-laws after his proxy in Harare forgot to show up to an important meeting. Needless to say, after fulfilling the betrothal terms of traditional law they were finally married under American law and now have two beautiful children.

I'm not sure if my friends' children will be raised in such a way that they too will feel obligated to observe African customs when they prepare for marriage. American society may have so influenced them that they may view those arrangements as geographically bound or optional. Indeed, countless laws relating to social customs, civic responsibility, and even religious practices change and vanish over time. The Italian military can no longer press people into carrying their luggage; in many (not all) societies an adulterous woman would not face stoning; a Jewish worshipper no longer slaughters animals to atone for sins; and the debate among rabbis about tithing food seasonings appears to have dissipated. The only law that defies fluctuation is God's covenant law as defined in the Ten Commandments. For the remainder of this book, we will mine the pages of the New Testament to rediscover the wonderful truths about a God of love who has empowered us to love Him back as we enter into covenant with Him.

---

[1] See comment by C. S. Keener, *The IVP Bible Background Commentary: New Testament* (Downers Grove, Ill.: InterVarsity Press, 1993), p. 60: "Roman soldiers had the legal right to impress the labor, work animal or substance of local residents (cf. Mark 15:21)."

[2] This is similar to the flexibility that some governments still extend to Muslim communities, allowing them to implement certain elements of Sharia. Also, many independent Jewish courts existed during the early days of America.

[3] See Anthony J. Saldarini, "Sanhedrin," in David Noel Freedman, ed., *Eerdmans Dictionary of the Bible* (Grand Rapids: Eerdmans, 2000), pp. 1166, 1167.

[4] *Ibid.*, p. 1167.

[5] We will discuss this in more detail in the section on rabbinic law.

[6] See John M. Lundquist, "Temple," in *Eerdmans Dictionary of the Bible*, pp. 1280-1284.

[7] See Hector Avalos, "Leprosy," in *Eerdmans Dictionary of the Bible*, p. 801.

[8] Keener reports that the rabbis "generally considered themselves spiritual heirs of the Pharisees" (p. 108).

[9] Leslie J. Hoppe, "Ten Commandments," in *Eerdmans Dictionary of the Bible*, p. 1285.

CHAPTER 2

Christ and the Law of Moses

I have many fond memories of my early life in South Norwood, a district in the southernmost section of London, England. I still remember the first day my mother took me to Portland Infant School. I had just turned 4, and it was to be my first time outside of her watchful care. My sister Karen was already there, and Vanessa—another sister—had survived her two years and had moved on to junior school. I didn't see Karen until lunch—actually, although it was lunchtime we called it dinner. We weren't seated at the same table, but just seeing her eased my anxiety. Some days at lunch I noticed that Karen and I had something different on our plates than the other children. Everyone had meat, but we had a huge chunk of cheese. Quickly I learned that those were pork days.

After two years in infant school, it was time to join Vanessa and Karen in junior school. By now my parents did not have to give a blanket directive to the school administration. We were old enough to speak for ourselves. On the days that products from a pig appeared on the menu, we simply said, "No meat, please," and received a piece of that famous cheddar cheese. I must confess that I did not always care for cheese. Some Fridays when the school served the traditional bangers, beans, and chips, I conveniently forgot to say "no meat" so that I would have an excuse to sink my teeth into the forbidden sausage. What I didn't count on was the extent of my mother's influence.

One day, as I prepared to do what I knew was unlawful, Mrs. Thomas, who was busy with something else, caught the scene out of the corner of her eye and shouted "Stop! That's Mrs. Burton's son—he doesn't eat pork!" Mrs. Thomas wasn't a Seventh-day Adventist, but she knew what we were supposed to stand for. I can still see that look of disappointment and reprimand in her face as she took my plate from her colleague and carefully placed an oversized piece of cheddar in the opening that I had envisioned being filled with two greasy sausages.

Dietary taboos were not the only things that made me aware of how different I was from my peers. My neighborhood offered a number of social opportunities for youth. I remember Tuesday Club and Thursday Club put on by the London City Mission. We would have time to sing choruses and do quizzes and crafts; we even had opportunities to win prizes. Many of the children in the community went to them—both churched and unchurched. As we got older, however, another club began to draw my peers' attention. It didn't focus on spiritual renewal, but provided opportunities for dancing to the latest hits and playing darts, snooker, and table football. It also introduced many of my friends to cigarettes and other vices.

By this time I knew better than to ask my parents' permission to join my friends for their weekly Friday night outings. It wasn't just that the winter discos took place during Sabbath hours—I knew enough about the church's standards to discern what their answer would have been. Fortunately we had great youth leadership in the church I attended, and we started our own club on Saturday nights during which we enjoyed the pool, darts, and table football in a smoke-free atmosphere in which we could conduct conversations without competing with deafening music.

Another area that reminded me of my "difference" was adornment. My parents were not too fussy about our desire to wear fashionable clothes. I still remember my first pair of three-button bell-bottoms that I proudly wore with either my black platform shoes or brown wedges. I even smile when I think about my pink Ben Sherman shirt with button-down collars and my Gabicci pullover that I wore with Farah slacks. My parents had no problem with them. However, when it came to certain items of jewelry, they drew a definite line.

I recall the day one of my good friends showed up to school with a shiny gold stud in his freshly pierced left ear. He was an overnight sensation! At that time in my social environment a pierced ear was a sign of toughness. My friend was officially a "lad." Yearning for some of the popularity he attracted, I garnered the courage to solicit my mother's permission to put a stud in my ear. She never forbade me, but the tone in her voice when she granted her permission was enough to let me know that I needed to forget my fascination for the fad in a hurry!

Whereas practices pertaining to diet, entertainment, and dress were governed by a written code that has helped to shape Adventist culture, other unwritten cultural norms also carried authoritative force. One was the practice of fasting on the first Sabbath of the quarter. Our parents never required us to join them, and would prepare a packed lunch for us while they joined the other fasters in the sanctuary for prayer and singing.

As we transitioned to our teen years, the adults' ascetic discipline fascinated the youth, and some of us made a pact to join them in the next Sabbath fast. It was my first experience with fasting, and what a lesson it was! The more I tried not to think about food, the hungrier I got. My friends and I literally counted down the seconds to sunset so that we could sink our teeth into the scrumptious pastries that the saintly Nanny Smith lovingly baked for us each week.

"Parental" Influence

As I reflect on the distinctive Adventist regulations that shaped my outlook on life, I am reminded that a religious worldview also shaped the life of the earthly Jesus. He was born into a particular religious context in which well-defined laws had informed a people's way of life for more than a millennium. God's special servant, Moses, had delivered those divine laws to His people, and they were supposed to serve as a blueprint for what it meant to live life in covenant with God. The fact that the death of Jesus would significantly alter the way in which one viewed those laws in the scheme of salvation in no way affected His commitment to honor them during His earthly sojourn.

While some Christians have taught that Jesus resisted Mosaic law, the biblical testimony gives a very different account. In fact, it appears as if the Godhead took special care to confirm the spiritual quality of the couple entrusted with the heavy responsibility to parent the Son of God. Matthew describes Joseph, Jesus' surrogate father, as a "righteous man" (Matt. 1:19). It is more than an honorific title but spoke to the very character of David's descendant. His righteousness was not merely manifested by external conformity to a set of rules, but he obviously knew the heart of God.

We clearly see Joseph's uprightness in the scandal surrounding Mary's premarital pregnancy. As we discussed in the previous chapter, the Mosaic law stipulated that a woman who violated a wedding contract should be publicly executed (even if engaged). Joseph would have been within his rights to initiate the stoning of Mary. However, the Bible states that his first response was to "divorce her quietly" (verse 19, NIV). He was willing to extend grace to his betrothed. His heart for God is also seen in the fact that after the Lord confirmed Mary's apparently bizarre story, Joseph submissively went ahead with the wedding plans. For the sake of God's ultimate plan, he was willing to have others believe that he had prematurely consummated his marriage. It was this man of grace and integrity whom the incarnated Son of God would first call "Abba."

The same pious spirit that led Joseph to submission also dwelled in the heart of Mary. When Gabriel gloriously appeared to the frightened young woman, who may still have been in her teenage years, he comforted and affirmed her with the words "Do not be afraid, Mary, for you have found favor with God" (Luke 1:30). The affirmation echoes the one bestowed on Noah, who, in the midst of a perverse and recalcitrant generation, also "found favor in the sight of the Lord" (Gen. 6:8).

Mary was by no means a random choice; neither was she programmed for the role before birth, as taught in the Koran and the Catholic doctrine of the Immaculate Conception. She was a loyal Jew who was so serious about her covenant relationship with God that she caught His attention. Like Isaiah responding to the divine call for a faithful bearer of the word, she volunteered her will to God with the words "Here am I, the servant of the Lord; let it be with me according to your word" (Luke 1:38).

Similar to Joseph, Mary also realized that her reputation was on the line. Society would forever view her as a hormone-driven fiancé who did not have the patience or self-control to wait until the official marriage service. She knew that those who had jealously admired her humble piety would now spitefully accuse her of hypocrisy. Still she willingly submitted to God, recognizing that the sullying of her reputation was nothing when compared to the grand restoration that would come to humanity through the One who would call her "Ima."

Covenant Rituals

When Jesus finally made His visible entrance into our world, Joseph and Mary were fully aware of their religious responsibilities. Unmindful of His surroundings, the incarnated One through whom everything exists had no idea that eight days had already passed, and a skilled priest had come to His temporary residence to conduct a ritualistic surgery that would indicate His status as a son of the covenant. It was the day of His circumcision (Luke 2:21).

The rite of circumcision had its roots in the life of Abraham. Immediately after God changed his name from Abram, God commanded him:

"Throughout your generations every male among you shall be circumcised when he is eight days old" (Gen. 17:12). The removal of the genital foreskin was more than a mere tribal marking. God stated that "it shall be a sign of the covenant between me and you" (verse 11). So important was it that the Lord stipulated, "Any uncircumcised male who is not circumcised in the flesh of his foreskin shall be cut off from his people; he has broken my covenant" (verse 14). It probably explains why although Abraham was 99 at the time and his oldest son, Ishmael, was 13, they were compelled to undergo the ritual (see verses 23-27).

As a reminder of the perpetual covenant, the law of Moses contained the simple statute: "On the eighth day the flesh of his foreskin shall be circumcised" (Lev. 12:3). Apparently God's people saw it as a twofold commandment that dealt not only with the "what" but the "when." In other words, it was not just about the surgical procedure but the day on which it was to be performed. When Jesus is criticized for healing on the Sabbath, He quickly retorted, "I performed one work, and all of you are astonished. Moses gave you circumcision . . . , and you circumcise a man on the sabbath. If a man receives circumcision on the sabbath in order that the law of Moses may not be broken, are you angry with me because I healed a man's whole body on the sabbath?" (John 7:20-23).

Given the significance of the ritual, Jewish culture expected Jesus' earthly parents as faithful Jews to fulfill the duty. Indeed, the fact that the circumcision also involved a naming ceremony made it even more special. The one who received the sign of the covenant was Himself the seal of the covenant who bore the name "Jesus"—Yahweh is salvation!

About a half century after the circumcision of Jesus, leading representatives of those who found salvation in Him convened in Jerusalem to discuss the applicability of circumcision for nondescendants of Abraham who had entered into covenant with Abraham's God (see Acts 15:1ff.). Some Pharisees who had accepted Christ felt that "it is necessary for them to be circumcised and ordered to keep the law of Moses" (verse 5). Peter countered with an appeal seemingly birthed from his own frustrating experience: "Why are you putting God to the test by placing on the neck of the disciples a yoke that neither our ancestors nor we have been able to bear? On the contrary, we believe that we will be saved through the grace of the Lord Jesus, just as they will" (verses 10, 11). Finally the delegates meeting in Jerusalem agreed that God accepted non-Jews into the covenant without them having to be circumcised.

Their ruling was in no way a command against circumcision—it was essentially an acknowledgment that human ritual does not evoke God's grace. In the very next chapter Paul recruits a young Christian named Timothy to his ministerial team. A son of a Jewish woman and Greek man, Timothy had never been circumcised. However, since the apostle's ministry took him to many sacred Jewish settings, he felt it best that Timothy embrace his mother's cultural heritage and undergo circumcision (Acts 16:1-3). He knew that circumcision was not necessary for salvation, but if it could help mission he had absolutely no problem with it.[1]

The One responsible for expanding the membership of those entering into covenant with God was to undergo another rite in His infancy. The same section of the Mosaic law that stipulated the day of His circumcision also declared the exact day that His parents should take Him to the Temple for the first time (Lev. 12:1-8). Everything depended on the ritual cleanliness of the mother, a condition determined by the gender of the child. If she bore a daughter, she would not be permitted to come in contact with any holy thing for 66 days. However, a male child affected her ritual status for only 33 days.

Luke reports, "When the time came for their purification according to the law of Moses, they brought him up to Jerusalem to present him to the Lord" (Luke 2:22). In his use of the plural Luke obviously refers to both Mary and Joseph. Although the passage in Leviticus refers to female uncleanliness, it appears that Joseph would have been deemed unclean by virtue of being in close proximity to his wife for the 33-day period. Nonetheless, it was a special event for the couple, not simply because Jesus was being *presented to* His heavenly Father, but as the firstborn He was being *sanctified for* His Father. Here again Luke quotes from the law of Moses that states, "Every firstborn male shall be designated as holy to the Lord" (verse 23; cf. Ex. 13:2).

The law also required a burnt offering on the day of presentation. Luke's allusion to what they brought is telling: "a pair of turtledoves or two young pigeons" (Luke 2:24). While he does not directly describe the content of their offering, the Mosaic code listed those categories as a substitutionary offering for those who could not afford the required gift of a 1-year-old lamb (see Lev. 12:6-8). Could this be an indication that Joseph and Mary were people of limited means for whom a "sacrifice" was really a *sacrifice?*[2] Of course, it is also possible that in the oral culture in which people memorized entire sections of Scripture, Luke was merely quoting a segment of the paragraph with the assumption that the people would have known the rest. Nonetheless, whatever the financial situation of Jesus' earthly parents, it is obvious that they were serious about raising Him as a son of the very covenant that He Himself had made with Israel.

Commemorative Holidays

Joseph and Mary's fidelity to the Mosaic law also evidences itself by their annual pilgrimages to Jerusalem for the Passover festival (Luke 2:41). The first major festival in the Jewish calendar year, it also marked the beginning of the seven-day Feast of Unleavened Bread. Passover for the Jews was the celebrative equivalent of Christmas in many contemporary traditions. It commemorated the day on which Yahweh's angel of death killed all the firstborn in Egypt but "passed over" the homes of the Israelites.

Apparently Jesus accompanied His surrogate parents on those annual visits. Luke informs us of one such visit when Jesus was 12 years old. Although the Bar Mitzvah ceremony for 13-year-old Jewish boys does not appear to have formalized until many centuries after Jesus' birth, it has traditionally been believed that this particular Passover visit symbolized His entrance into manhood.[3] Indeed, it was on this occasion that He first expressed an awareness of His divine identity (see verse 49).

Knowing the significance of the festival, Jesus' observance of Passover did not cease when He left His parents' home. It was on one of those visits at the commencement of His ministry that He chased corrupt traders from the Temple premises (John 2:13-22). One can only imagine the righteous indignation that had built up in His spirit through the years of seeing His heavenly Father's house transformed into a marketplace in which religious leaders exploited those who came to the Temple.

Jesus observed the Passover festival until the very end of His time on earth. Aware of His practice, when the time for the feast came around, His disciples instinctively asked, "Where do you want us to make the preparations for you to eat the Passover?" (Matt. 26:17). The question itself suggests that it was a custom they regularly observed during the few years during which He had mentored them. Although nothing in the Bible suggests that Passover observance is obligatory to Christians, Jesus' final words at the final Passover feast indicate that there will be a future opportunity to celebrate with Jesus Himself: "I have eagerly desired to eat this Passover with you before I suffer; for I tell you, I will [never eat it again] until it is fulfilled in the kingdom of God" (Luke 22:15, 16).

Passover (which was actually the beginning of the seven-day Feast of Unleavened Bread) was just one of three major holidays that all Jews were expected to observe. Exactly 50 days after Passover came the festival known as *Shevuot*, which we know by its Greek-derived name, Pentecost. The rabbis believed that it was the day that Yahweh gave the law to Moses.[4] While the Gospels have no record of Jesus observing Pentecost, the circumstances surrounding the outpouring of the Holy Spirit in Acts could not be coincidental. Here we see Jesus instructing the disciples not to leave Jerusalem until they receive baptism with the Holy Spirit (see Acts 1:4, 5).

At the original Pentecost, when God gave the Ten Commandments to Moses, the Bible tells us, "Now Mount Sinai was wrapped in smoke, because the Lord had *descended* upon it in *fire*; the smoke went up like the smoke of a kiln, while the whole mountain *shook violently*" (Ex. 19:18). The images of divine descent, fire, and fierce movement also appear in the second Pentecost: "And suddenly *from heaven there came* a sound like *the rush of a violent wind*, and it filled the entire house where they were sitting. Divided tongues, as of *fire*, appeared among them, and a tongue rested on each one of them" (Acts 2:2, 3). Passover received renewed significance with the death of Jesus; and the same Spirit that visited God's messenger Moses fell upon the bearers of the gospel message.

The third major holiday season in the Mosaic law commenced with the solemn day known as Yom Kippur (the Day of Atonement) and ended with Sukkôth (the Feast of Booths). Yom Kippur was probably the most solemn day of the Jewish year, and indicated the removal of all sin from Israel. Sukkôth was another reminder of the Israelites' experience wandering in the wilderness and commemorated their nomadic years when they lived in portable tents. While the New Testament says nothing about Jesus observing Yom Kippur, it does inform us that He did participate in Sukkôth.

We learn two interesting lessons from John's account of Jesus and the Feast of Booths (John 7:1ff). First is the observation that He was not under any compulsion to attend the official celebration of the feast in Jerusalem. Although cajoled by His brothers, He initially refused to acquiesce because He knew that it would put His life in danger. If observance of Sukkôth were a mandatory religious obligation for all under the Mosaic covenant, then surely Jesus would not have allowed death threats to keep Him away from the festivities. From this incident, we also gather that although Jesus was not compelled by divine law to attend, He appears to have had a desire to participate. Indeed, not long after He told His brothers He would not go, He changed His mind and attended the feast in disguise.

The New Testament has no indication that those under the new covenant are obligated to keep the major Jewish feasts, neither does the Bible teach that there is—or ever has been—anything salvific about them. However, it does appear that the Jewish calendar was the framework for the Christian year. Even Luke's mainly Gentile audience would have known the period indicated by "Feast of Unleavened Bread" when some suffered persecution (Acts 12:1-4). Paul tells the Corinthians that he would remain at Ephesus until Pentecost (1 Cor. 16:5-8). He also waited until the Feast of Unleavened Bread ended before sailing from Philippi to Troas (Acts 20:6). And Luke once more refers to the Day of Atonement (the Fast) to indicate the time of year when the weather became difficult for traveling (Acts 27:9). While it is clear that the observance of such days was not a test of faith for early Christians, it is also evident that they were fully aware of their religious significance and, like Jesus, probably viewed them as holidays (in much the same way as moderns view Easter, Christmas, Thanksgiving, etc.).

Perspective on Law

The circumstance surrounding Jesus' change of mind about going to Jerusalem for the Feast of Booths helps us to discern how Jesus viewed the Mosaic law as a whole. We cannot deny the fact that the New Testament depicts Him as a law-observant Jew. In fact, very early in His ministry He lays out His agenda as it relates to the Mosaic law: "Do not think that I have come to abolish the law or the prophets; I have come not to abolish but to fulfill" (Matt. 5:17). It's almost as if He is forewarning His disciples that some of the things He plans to do will appear to go against the law. However, His real intention is not to negate the law, but to highlight its true meaning.

We see this powerfully illustrated in the account of the woman caught in adultery (John 8:1-11). In the previous chapter we briefly established that the woman had indeed violated the Mosaic law. The stoning that her accusers demanded was not based on kangaroo justice but was firmly grounded in their penal code. Nonetheless, when they sought Jesus' endorsement to carry out a punishment that they were fully authorized to administer, He countered with a soul-penetrating response that led to the woman's acquittal.

It is easy to interpret Jesus' response as one that went against the law of Moses. However, a straight reading of the text does not support that view. From the outset He offers His qualified endorsement to those who would pit Him against Moses: "Let anyone among you who is without sin be the first to throw a stone at her" (verse 7). Notice that He does not say she should not be stoned—she was indeed guilty of a crime and was fully deserving of the punishment that faced her. Notwithstanding, the hypocritical motives of those who sought "justice" disqualified them from administering it.[5]

Even Jesus' affirmation of her acquittal is in harmony with the Mosaic law. The law clearly stipulated two or three witnesses before the death sentence could be administered (Deut. 17:6). If the criterion were met, the woman's future would have still been in jeopardy. However, the fact that all those who had pointed a finger at her had disappeared into the darkness of their own deviances meant that the same law that would have caused her death had now granted her another chance at life. In His actions Jesus demonstrated the true purpose of any divinely derived law. Godly laws are not meant to evoke anger and spiteful revenge in the heart of the legalist, but to illuminate a path that leads to abundant life and wholeness. Hence His admonition to the acquitted: "Go your way, and from now on do not sin again" (verse 11).

Another place that Jesus appears to contradict the law of Moses is Matthew 19:1-9 when He debates divorce and remarriage with some Pharisees. In response to their question regarding grounds for divorce, Jesus refers them to the Genesis creation account to establish the permanency of marriage. They probably could not wait for Him to finish so that they could pounce on Him with a "gotcha" text that would for once give them an upper hand over Him. Referring to Deuteronomy 24:1-4, they retort, "Why then did Moses command us to give a certificate of dismissal and divorce her?" (Matt. 19:7).

Again their attempt to pit Jesus against Moses would not work. Jesus had no problem taking those learned men back to school as He challenged their nuanced use of the word "command." Both Jesus and they were fully aware that no text says "Thou shalt divorce thy wife!" In fact, the very text to which they referred is structured as a scenario: "Suppose a man enters into marriage with a woman, but she does not please him because he finds something objectionable about her, and so he writes her a certificate of divorce, puts it in her hands, and sends her out of his house" (Deut. 24:1). The passage *assumes* that divorces take place but does not demand that they *should*. Hence Jesus' careful correction of their choice of words as He reiterates His original point: "It was because you were so hard-hearted that Moses *allowed you* to divorce your wives, but from the beginning it was not so" (Matt. 19:8).[6]

On the surface, it does appear as if Jesus contradicts Moses. He clearly states that what Moses' allowed was not in harmony with the original ideal. Nonetheless, He is also aware that Moses did not pen this statute to counter the very One who supervised him as he wrote Israel's legal code. The very law illustrates the grace of a God who understands that people who possess free choice may sometimes make decisions that go against the divine intent. Had Jesus stopped with the contrasting statement, it would have been fair to accuse Him of going against the Mosaic law. However, He continues, "And I say to you, whoever divorces his wife, except for unchastity, and marries another commits adultery" (verse 9). With those words He acknowledges that portions of the Mosaic code sought to accommodate context-specific social realities, and although they may not reflect God's original intent, they did help to bring stability in a community affected by sin.

We see Jesus' willingness to endorse context-based sections of the Mosaic law also demonstrated in the event involving the Temple tax that we discussed in the previous chapter. On one level, we could argue that the issue should not even have been debatable, since the Temple tax was an obligatory levy on all Israelite men that exempted only the Levites (Deut. 10:9). However, Jesus believed that His divine Sonship automatically excluded Him from payment (Matt. 17:25-27). Nonetheless, He did not feel that it was a fight worth having, and utilized His divine power to secure the exact funds for the tax collectors. This incident, along with the others, shows that throughout His life Jesus voluntarily submitted Himself to the Mosaic law.

Conclusion

The present chapter has provided a unique look into the life of Jesus the Jew. After centuries of Christian anti-Semitism, it is not uncommon for those who claim to follow the Messiah to overlook the very faith that nurtured our incarnated Lord. Despite their very public failures, our Jewish forebears were still the people of the promise to whom God had entrusted His laws and covenants. Given this reality, we should expect the divine Son of God to enter the world among "His own." The carefully chosen Joseph and Mary ensured that their child would undergo all the rituals required of the son of the covenant.

As He developed intellectually, physically, spiritually, and socially (Luke 2:52), Jesus learned to cherish the culture that shaped Him. During

His public ministry He did not cease to observe publically the major feasts that commemorated significant events in Israel's collective history. Neither did He shirk from paying a required tax that He could have made a case for exemption. He was not one to dismantle a legal system that served a righteous purpose, but consistently lived under the terms of the Mosaic law while taking every opportunity to share the spirit of grace that should possess every divine law.

Jesus' attitude toward the religious laws that shaped His community was very different from mine in my formative years. He was not one to violate the edges of the moral code or to seek loopholes that would allow Him to live free from law. It was not until the end of my second decade on earth that I began seriously to consider the purpose of the customs and laws that we hold dear as Seventh-day Adventists.

From a child's perspective, it was all about doing or not doing things to gain God's favor. However, as I matured, I understood that any divinely originated law has freedom as its ultimate goal. Rather than deprive me of greasy taste-good foods and mind-altering beverages, health laws free me to enjoy the fullness of life in several dimensions. Rather than limit my social options, guidelines on wholesome recreation allow me to engage in social activities that enhance true joy and builds up Christ. Rather than self-torment, spiritual discipline permits me to depend fully on God for His sustenance.

Jesus modeled this type of freedom throughout His earthly life. While others inadvertently violated the first commandment by placing the Mosaic law in place of the Lawgiver, Jesus demonstrated the true purpose of divine law as He pointed people to the God of grace who "did not send the Son into the world to condemn the world, but in order that the world might be saved through him" (John 3:17). God's covenant has always been about liberation, and even through the Mosaic law Christ has made this known.

---

[1] See Allan R. Bevere, "Circumcision," in *Eerdmans Dictionary of the Bible*, p. 256.

[2] See C. S. Keener, *IVP Bible Background Commentary*, p. 194.

[3] See Keener, p. 195, who compares it to a "Roman coming-of-age" ritual.

[4] See Frank H. Gorman, "Pentecost," in *Eerdmans Dictionary of the Bible*, p. 1027.

[5] See my discussion in Keith Burton, *Compassion of the Christ* (Grantham, Eng.: Stanborough Press, 2004), pp. 51, 52.

[6] See discussion in Keith Augustus Burton, "A Christian Theology of Divorce and Remarriage," *Ministry*, April 2001, pp. 20-22.

CHAPTER 3

Christ and the Law of Religious Tradition

I don't remember the color of the cover (it could have been lime green), but I can vaguely recall the black binding that secured the spine on the letter-sized lithographed book that bore the intriguing title *The Sabbath Even Message*. It was probably the first time that "dissidents" from America had disturbed the relative tranquillity that characterized the Croydon Seventh-day Adventist Church, located in a London suburb. They seemed to have a copy of their "new light" document for everyone, and although never permitted an opportunity to present their material inside the sanctuary, they sure garnered a crowd outside the church building after the "MV" meeting.[1]

Our American visitors said they were Seventh-day Adventists, but the message they advocated was obvious heresy to the elders who engaged them in biblical debate. If God wanted Adventists all over the globe to keep the Sabbath at the exact time it fell in Israel—regardless of the time zone—then surely there must be biblical evidence, the unpersuaded elders reasoned. Their argument seemed reasonable to me, and although I carefully reread and held on to my personal copy of the book for years afterward, I was never convinced by their argument (even though it was obvious that they themselves were staunch in their position). I especially did not believe that rejecting their interpretation of Scripture would exclude me from a place in Christ's kingdom.

About a decade later I was a first-year theology major at Oakwood College (now Oakwood University). I had not too long embraced my ministerial calling after a sojourn in the same wilderness made famous by the prodigal. Now with renewed vigor, I aimed to be the best Christian in the world. I guess my overzealousness must have manifested itself in an unconscious way, because I soon received an invitation to a special Bible study being held at an off-campus location on Sunday mornings. The person conducting the study appeared pious and sincere, and modeled the perfect profile to which I aspired.

But I attended only one meeting. Although billed as such, it wasn't really a Bible study. It's not that it didn't use the Bible, but there were a number of other books and pamphlets that served the purposes of the one leading the discussion. Those extrabiblical materials might have piqued the curiosity of others, but had the opposite effect on my inquiring mind—the truth is I was totally overwhelmed! I cannot recollect how long the study lasted, but I do know that at the end of the intensive session I remained unconvinced and made no firm commitment to attend future sessions. Unfortunately the friend who invited me soon left the Seventh-day Adventist Church (along with his siblings) and joined a Sundaykeeping church, which they believed liberated them from "Adventist legalism." When I heard of their change of allegiance, I could not help reflecting on that Sunday-morning "Bible" study, in which the presentation of the gospel was anything but "good news."

Probably a dozen years after that experience I found myself facing the opposite direction of the classroom than I did in my days as a student. I had recently finished my Doctor of Philosophy degree in New Testament studies and had been invited to my alma mater to help "sound the call" of the young men and women in the ministerial program. My teaching and mentoring responsibilities extended to the broader student body, as I taught a section of Life and Teachings of Jesus and served as faculty sponsor for several campus clubs. Everything appeared to be running smoothly until a charismatic self-supporting evangelist came to town.

Student attendance at the influential evangelist's meetings began to swell, and I felt a duty to assess the situation. Arriving at the location early, I took a place in the middle of the auditorium. As I waited to hear what the man had to say, I tried to have an open mind. I could have excused the fact that the evangelist spoke with authority about the "original" meaning of a New Testament term that was not even in the passage upon which he expounded (I hear well-intended preachers making such errors all the time). However, what disturbed me most was the grace-devoid content of the message that he delivered in such a charismatic way that many in the congregation appeared to be imprisoned in the speaker's hypnotic grip.

Sadly, at the conclusion of the series the talk around campus was not about how many people he had added to the church through baptism, but about several students so beguiled by the "evangelist's" message that they chose to withdraw from their education. His destructive teaching has had lasting effects to this very day. Some of his converts have never finished their degrees, and many have lived to regret their decision. Others have come to realize that the yoke placed upon them was too heavy a burden to bear, and instead of coming back to Jesus, have turned their back on the church—a classic case of "throwing out the baby with the bathwater"! But a defiant "remnant" continued to refuse to allow the gospel to judge the content of their esoteric teachings as they sought to spread the "bad news" about a Deity who has set the bar so high that only a talented few can surmount it.

The Truth About the Teachers

I honestly don't believe that many of the religious leaders who promote a narrow view of the gospel do so with ill intention. Their zeal often results from a desire to see a community of people whose deeds are pleasing to God. That was definitely the case with the scribes and Pharisees that we encounter in the Gospels and the book of Acts. Although it is possible that the scribes were an independent group,[2] it is more likely that they were a scholarly subset of the Pharisees tasked with the arduous duty of dissecting the law. That appears to be Luke's understanding of the relationship between the two when he refers to "certain scribes of the Pharisees' group" (Acts 23:9).

We have no extant account of the origin of the Pharisees, but they had already emerged as a developed group toward the middle of the second century B.C. when Greece's dominance as a world power had begun waning. It is believed that they had their roots in the Hasidim, another pious group whose origins are unknown.[3] The Hasidim ("holy ones") had joined with the rebel group known as the Maccabees to liberate the Jews from their imperial Greek overlords. After the Jews achieved independence, we hear little about the Hasidim, and the Pharisees take the center stage as the epitome of Jewish piety. Many scholars have associated their name with the Hebrew term *paras,* which means "to separate." They were the ones supposed to set themselves apart from evil influences so that they could lead all Jews to a separate existence and regain Yahweh's favor. In the postbiblical era the rabbis would eventually assume the mission of the Pharisees.[4]

The multiple harsh statements about the "scribes and Pharisees" in the Gospels have led most Christians to view them in a negative light. We lightly use the term *Pharisee* as a byword for "legalist," and often see no redeeming quality in this Jewish subset that appears to oppose Jesus' every move. However, before our traditional stereotypes lead us prematurely to cast a guilty verdict on *all* Pharisees, it may be wise to take another look at the Gospel witness.

From a relational perspective, it is obvious that a number of Pharisees admired Jesus. In spite of their objection to His association with religious outcasts, some even invited Him to dine with them on occasion (e.g., Luke 7:36; 11:37). One Pharisee appeared to be especially close to Him—Nicodemus. A member of the Sanhedrin, he had found himself attracted to Jesus from the inception of His public ministry (John 3:1). While not invited to serve in Jesus' inner circle, it does appear that he was a silent follower. In fact, even as the disciples hid in fear after the Crucifixion, it was Nicodemus along with Joseph of Arimethea—also a member of the Sanhedrin—who claimed the body of Jesus (John 19:38, 39; cf. Luke 23:50-53).

It also seems that many may have viewed Jesus Himself as an honorary Pharisee. Of course, nowhere does the New Testament designate Him thusly. However, we find a number of times when He is called "Rabbi" (e.g., Matt. 26:25, 49; Mark 9:5; 11:21; John 3:2). Whereas the term *rabbi* would not take on an official connotation until after the destruction of the Temple in A.D. 70,[5] the Gospels suggest that it is the title that scribes and Pharisees preferred. Jesus chastised them about their fixation on the title when He said, "They love to have the place of honor at banquets and the best seats in the synagogues, and to be greeted with respect in the marketplaces, and to have people call them *rabbi*" (Matt. 23:6, 7).

We should not see Jesus' reprimand as a blanket denouncement of the Pharisees. In fact, His words follow a strong endorsement of their role when He states, "The scribes and Pharisees sit on Moses' seat; therefore, do whatever they teach you and follow it" (verses 2, 3). Here Jesus affirms the need for religious teachers academically prepared to explain the teachings of the Bible. As we see in the Sermon on the Mount, He Himself took the time to model God-centered methods of interpretation to His disciples. That is not to say that only those who have undergone advanced studies have the ability to teach the Word, but it does call for a high level of proficiency on the part of those who "sit on Moses' seat."

Adding to the Word

Jesus' interactions with the Pharisees clearly show us that His problem was not with their assumed or appointed roles, but with the fact that "they do not practice what they teach" (verse 3). Somehow, in trying to get people to keep the law of Moses, they missed the mark by piling on a mountain of human-made regulations that only served the purpose of burying the very laws they sought to preserve. One of two rabbinic schools headquartered in Jerusalem most likely collated the laws espoused by the Pharisees.

Founded by the biblical scholars Hillel and Shammai, the schools had a deep history that Jewish tradition traces to Ezra.[6] Supposedly upon his return to Jerusalem from captivity in Babylon Ezra founded a seminary to ensure that Judah would remain faithful to the law. He was the first in a line of scholars known as the *sopherim* who orally transmitted the teachings and interpretations of the law. After the Maccabean wars, rather than having one teacher head the school, the Jewish leadership decided that the students would be best served by having the perspectives of two teachers called *zugoth*, the Hebrew word for "pairs." A total of five *zugoth* headed the school in succession, and Hillel and Shammai, who were active during the time of Jesus, were the final pair.

The "pairs" system gave way to the era of the *tannaim,* in which the number of teachers increased. *Tannaim* is the plural form of the Hebrew word *tana*, which we can translate either as "teacher" or "repeater." They reflected either the conservative teachings of Rabbi Shammai or the more liberal interpretations of Rabbi Hillel. The apostle Paul's teacher, Gamaliel I, numbered among the *tannaim,* belonged to the more liberal tradition aligned with his grandfather, Hillel.[7] Through the years the *tannaim* developed several principles for interpreting Scripture that led to the various rabbinic laws.

The establishment of extrabiblical rules for regulating religious activities is not inherently wrong. In fact, Paul's first letter to the church in Corinth contains several. For instance, Paul's teaching on a believer staying married to a nonbelieving spouse has no biblical precedent, but reflects his reasoning that one made the other holy (1 Cor. 7:12). Another case involves the prohibition on a woman worshipping without a head covering, a decision simply based on "custom" (1 Cor. 11:16). Additionally the rule that wives should not interrupt the church service derived from common consensus (1 Cor. 14:33, 34). Paul's introduction of unprecedented regulations is merely a recognition that we cannot always find an exact scripture to address changing circumstances. It is at such times that we can articulate and apply godly principles. However, we must take great care to ensure that such culturally bound concepts never become so authoritative that they eclipse or even replace the spirit of the revealed law of God.

The extent to which people elevated the law of the Pharisees to canonical status becomes evident in a number of places in the Gospels. In fact, when they noticed a violation, they were bold enough to cite the source of their discontent. We see this in the question posed to Jesus in Matthew's Gospel: "Why do your disciples break the tradition of the elders? For they do not wash their hands before they eat" (Matt. 15:2). Nowhere does the Bible forbid people from eating before washing their hands. This particular law was grounded in an oral legal tradition that had the force of law.

While some good health reasons exist for washing hands before eating, sanitary concerns was not the reason behind the prohibition. It was really about ceremonial cleanliness. The Pharisees were concerned that in going about their day-to-day business, it was highly probable that people would touch something handled by an unclean or defiled individual. If those persons ate without washing their hands, the contamination would transfer to the food, and the food would consequently be defiled. Mark's account of the incident elaborates that the practice of purification extended to "the washing of cups, pots, and bronze kettles" (Mark 7:4).

Jesus does not respond directly to the Pharisees' question, but instead poses one obviously intended to get them to refocus: "And why do you break the commandment of God for the sake of your tradition?" (Matt. 15:3). Showing His familiarity with the intricate details of their tradition, He provides a concrete example: "For God said, 'Honor your father and your mother,' and 'Whoever speaks evil of father or mother must surely die.' But you say that whoever tells father or mother, 'Whatever support you might have had from me is given to God,' then that person need not honor the father" (verses 4, 5).

Voiding the Word

The implications of such a contradiction are clear to Jesus: "So, for the sake of your tradition, you make void the word of God" (verse 6). In their effort to be righteous they had resorted to a self-righteousness devoid of any godly characteristics. Instead of serving the purpose of walking around the law so as not to violate it, keeping *their* commandments (*halakhah*) resulted in them trampling over the very law of love that God had given to Israel. Hence Jesus' harsh denouncement on the legalists: "You hypocrites!

Isaiah prophesied rightly about you when he said: 'This people honors me with their lips, but their hearts are far from me; in vain do they worship me, teaching human precepts as doctrines'" (verses 7-9).

Before Jesus voiced His analysis, it probably never even dawned on the Pharisees that the elevation of their commandments had in effect nullified God's commandments. They had become so caught up in the minutia that they had totally lost sight of what really mattered.[8] As self-appointed doorkeepers for the kingdom they had developed their own list of entrance requirements. Jesus exposes their apostasy in the extended denouncement that comes several chapters later: "But woe to you, scribes and Pharisees, hypocrites! For you lock people out of the kingdom of heaven. For you do not go in yourselves, and when others are going in, you stop them" (Matt. 23:13). They were hurting the very people whom they purported to help. Jesus' indictment did not stop there. Hoping to let them reflect on the errors of their ways, He continues, "Woe to you, scribes and Pharisees, hypocrites! For you cross sea and land to make a single convert, and you make the new convert twice as much a child of hell as yourselves" (verse 15).

It is probably because He knew that people had become confused by the Pharisees' teaching that He summoned the crowd after exposing the religious leaders and made the pronouncement "Listen and understand: it is not what goes into the mouth that defiles a person, but it is what comes out of the mouth that defiles" (Matt. 15:10, 11). As it relates to things spiritual, we must place everything in its proper perspective. If people reduce their spiritual life to a list of laborious and esoteric rules, they have absolutely no way to appreciate the God of love and grace for who He is. Emphasizing the washing of hands is good, but when it becomes a test of fellowship, the practice slides into the realm of the idolatrous. Those truly concerned with living a life pleasing to God will be more concerned about the spiritual condition of their heart. After all, what is the spiritual benefit of eating right if the words from a person's mouth are spiteful or deceitful?

Interestingly, some have taken the very words that Jesus used to rebuke the Pharisees to create their own human-made commandment about what food the Bible permits for consumption. They note that in some translations of Mark's extended account of this incident, he does not simply report what Jesus says about defilement, but he appears to add an interpretive comment: "Thus he declared all foods clean" (Mark 7:19). Based on this alleged parenthetical statement, some Christians believe that we are free to eat anything we want. One commentator even gets quite specific with his declaration that "pigs, dogs, bats, owls and so on are now 'clean,' or acceptable to eat."[9]

I would be the first to admit that if this were indeed an interpretive comment, when read in isolation it does seem to lift the ban on foods deemed unclean from before the Flood. However, we must note two observations before reaching a verdict. First is the context of the statement. The issue under debate does not concern whether a person can eat clean or unclean foods, but whether *clean* food eaten with unwashed hands is defiled (cf. Mark 7:18; Matt. 15:20). I don't know any scholar from any ideological persuasion who would even suggest that the issue involved nonkosher food. The passage has no logical link between dirty hands and the banning of biblical taboos against certain foods.

Second, and most important, is the fact that when reading the text in the original language, that clause has no term that can be directly translated "declared." Those who render the text this way do so *after* determining that the clause is Mark's interpretive comment and not the actual words of Jesus. However, some translators stick to a literal translation of the text: "Are you thus without understanding also? Do you not perceive that whatever enters a man from outside cannot defile him, because it does not enter his heart but his stomach, and is eliminated, *thus purifying all foods*" (Mark 7:18, 19, NKJV)?

When seen as the very words of Jesus, the notion that He calls for the nullification of the food laws is not even an option. He essentially clarifies that food eaten with unwashed hands goes through the digestive system in the same manner as food consumed with sanitized hands. It has absolutely no effect on your spiritual health. In other words, true righteousness is a matter of the heart and not the stomach. It is in being, not in doing, that a person embraces this status.

An Excessive Righteousness

This practical teaching would not have been new to Jesus' disciples. The very fact that they even ate without washing their hands in the presence of the Pharisees is enough to indicate their liberation from human rules that only made their lives miserable. Their association with Christ was leading them to refocus on the God of grace who calls us to a relationship built on love, not fear. It is one in which people understand that the purpose of all divinely derived commandments is not to restrict but to liberate. As John would later testify, God's commandments are never burdensome (1 John 5:3), and when we are truly in harmony with them we will never have feelings of complexity or confusion. When *keeping* the commandments in the way that God intended, the person of faith will be at peace. Hence the psalmist proclaims, "Great peace have they which love thy law: and nothing shall offend them" (Ps. 119:165, KJV).

With their fixation on an ever-growing body of legal codes, the Pharisees were pushing themselves further away from the very righteousness they sought to attain. Given this reality, one wonders why Jesus would tell His disciples, "Unless your righteousness exceeds that of the scribes and Pharisees, you will never enter the kingdom of heaven" (Matt. 5:20). His perplexing statement has led some to believe that Jesus is inviting them to out-Pharisee the Pharisees. However, it could be the case only if He endorsed the laborious path upon which the Pharisees traveled. In a very provocative way, it is a tongue-in-cheek statement in which Jesus actually denounces the superficiality of the pharisaical method of gaining God's favor. By burdening themselves and others with a plethora of minutia, they have in effect created a system of religion drastically different from the one that God revealed through Moses at Sinai.

So what is the *excessive* righteousness that Jesus promotes? The passage from Isaiah that He quotes during the controversy over hand washing sums it up: "These people . . . honor me with their lips, but their hearts are far from me" (Isa. 29:13, NIV). The self-righteous among the Pharisees were very good in paying God lip service. They talked a very good talk and had the masses fooled into believing that their external religiosity guaranteed them a place in the kingdom. However, God is not impressed with mere ritual and ceremony—He seeks hearts that yearn to be in communion with Him. He needs people who are not so enamored by the law that they have lost sight of the Lawgiver.

A legalistic mentality that purports an exclusive path to the kingdom is not limited only to the extremist Pharisees in Scripture. Another example appears in a most unusual place—the story of the woman at the well (John 4:1-42). By all indications, the unnamed woman did not appear to be overly religious. In fact, judging by her polyandrous lifestyle, she may not have been religious at all. Thus it makes it even more shocking when in the midst of her conversation with Jesus, she challenges Him to a religious debate by saying, "Our ancestors worshiped on this mountain, but you say that the place where people must worship is in Jerusalem" (verse 20). In contrasting the different places of worship, she's basically saying that her "denomination" is more authentic than His.

The tendency to feel spiritually secure because of denominational affiliation or an intellectual understanding of a body of doctrines is a stellar example of the type of righteousness that Jesus decries. It does not matter how much knowledge of biblical truth a group may espouse, mere membership in it does not give a person an automatic pass to the kingdom. As Jesus explained to the Samaritan woman, the Father is seeking true worshippers who will worship Him in spirit and truth (verses 23, 24). It is those who have invited the Holy Spirit into their lives and have asked Him to guide their every path as they pledge to go wherever He leads. They are not obsessed with memorizing volumes of supplementary rules, but feast on the Word and invite the Spirit to store it in their heart so that all of their actions will bring glory to the Almighty.

Conclusion

We have assessed the way in which humanly contrived religious rules often present a barrier to the gospel. Although many who espouse such regulations have good intentions, they are totally ignorant of God's intentions. The Pharisees believed that the development of minor laws would help the people to observe the major laws, but before long the minor became major. Unfortunately, the very teachers who could have helped to bring about genuine spiritual revival became the source of legalistic apostasy. Nowhere do we see their distance from the kingdom more clearly demonstrated than in their willingness to allow their own rules to overshadow the laws given to Israel through Moses. Sadly, such human-made commandments unintentionally make void the very law of God.

Interestingly, the same spirit behind the Pharisees' apostasy is present in the hearts and minds of those who may not necessarily display legalistic behavior but believe that their church affiliation affords them spiritual security. Replacing the divinely revealed code with relaxed rules is just as destructive as adding to it with restrictive ones. Both extremes amount to religious systems that rival the one revealed in Scripture. Christ calls all those who seek to lean on human systems to experience instead a true righteousness that does not depend on humanly contrived religious codes or a false security based on denominational affiliation, but rather the presence of the Holy Spirit in their heart.

A heart possessed by God's Spirit will automatically become a channel of God's love and grace. When a person's heart is right with God, they are able to fulfill His will without resorting to legalism. During my years in ministry I have witnessed countless expressions of such legalistic spirit. Some obvious cases involve church extremists who condemn people for not wearing hats in church or for eating cheese. But others are so subtle in their legalism that it is often not even noticed. I still remember the instance when a pastor advised a woman to withdraw her membership so that he could officiate over her marriage to a nonbeliever without violating the *Pastor's Manual*. As far as he was concerned, she could always get baptized again after the ceremony![10]

Godly derived laws were never intended to be flexible fodder for clever religious lawyers looking for loopholes and imagining new ways to manipulate their meaning. They were written in such clear terms that they are not even open to interpretation. When humans try to "help God out" by adding supplementary regulations or subtracting from or amending what has already been written, they are going down the same path as those Pharisees so obsessed by their own laws that they saw His as secondary. Christ's interactions with the Pharisees remind us that those who wish to follow God's law should do so on His terms and no other.

---

[1] MV is the abbreviation for Missionary Volunteers, the forerunner to the Adventist Youth Society.

[2] See Kim Paffenroth, "Scribes," in *Eerdmans Dictionary of the Bible*, p. 1173.

[3] See discussion in Steve Mason, "Pharisees," in *Eerdmans Dictionary of the Bible*, pp. 1043, 1044.

[4] *Ibid.*

[5] W. Dennis Tucker, Jr., "Rabbi," in *Eerdmans Dictionary of the Bible*, pp. 1105, 1106.

[6] Although some go as far back as Moses.

[7] W. E. Nunnally, "Gamaliel," in *Eerdmans Dictionary of the Bible*, pp. 481, 482.

[8] Ellen G. White, in *The Desire of Ages* (Mountain View, Calif.: Pacific Press Pub. Assn., 1898), comments: "While the people were occupied with trifling distinctions, and observances which God had not required, their attention was turned away from the great principles of His law" (p. 396).

[9] C. S. Keener, *IVP Bible Background Commentary*, p. 153.

[10] I know also of a member who requested disfellowship—rather than censorship—because it would place her on a faster track to rebaptism.

CHAPTER 4

Christ and the Law in the Sermon on the Mount

It was a typical gray London afternoon, and my best friend invited me to play on the flat roof of the home that sat atop his family's electronic shop. We were both 8 years old and totally naive about the racial undercurrents that formed the foundation of our fragile society. His father was preoccupied with customers when we entered the shop, and probably did not see us as we passed through the back door and ascended the stairs to the living quarters. We had been playing for about 15 minutes when his father took a break and spotted us on the roof. I was totally unprepared for what happened next.

Without warning, the father stormed toward us and grabbed me by the arm as he chastised his son for taking a Black person (he used another term) into his house. My heart pounded uncontrollably as a grown man dragged me down the stairs, pulled me through the store, and threw me out the front door while shouting insulting expletives. The next day in school, for the first time since we had known each other, my friend addressed me with the same derogatory term that I had heard his father use the day before. Needless to say, that was the end of our friendship, and from that day onward I had as much disdain for him as he apparently had for me.

Being awakened to my racialized society, I began to view my world in terms of "us" and "them." It didn't help that I was part of a very small minority with absolutely no representation—at that time—in the government, classroom, or police force. Thus I had seemingly nowhere to turn when the school bully—who also happened to be an expert boxer—decided that I was to be the object of his hatred for people with darkened skin. I still remember the day we engaged in scrappy combat, and the blood and bruises that led my normally peaceful father to chastise my brother for not coming to my assistance! Fortunately for me, my brother took Dad's advice, and when the two of us stood up to the bully and his gang of four,

I was never bothered again. Interestingly, we never even had to throw a punch.

Those who have never experienced such treatment may wonder why I never reported the bullying to an authority figure. Well, in my experience, authority figures were also a part of the problem. For instance, my woodwork teacher took pleasure in arbitrarily picking me out for corporal punishment. I have vivid memories of him locking my hand in a vise and giving me "six of the best" with a bamboo cane. My crime? Tardiness. I hated that man with a passion and rehearsed scenarios in my mind of how I was going to get him back in the future when nature had equalized our statures. I couldn't wait for the day!

By the time I finished high school, my anger (which was arguably justifiable or at the least explainable) was not directed just toward individuals but toward an entire system. I recall the evening a gang of police officers stopped me and accused me of stealing my own car. I was 18 at the time and knew that the officers had racially profiled me. They tried to incite me to violence, and when that did not work, they wrestled me to the ground, handcuffed me, threw me into the back of the police van, took me to the police station, and had me charged with assaulting a police officer in the execution of his duty—among other things. Fortunately, they were not successful in their effort to imprison me, and the Holy Spirit influenced the all-White jury to find me not guilty. It was the first time I had heard of such a verdict in an obviously racist case that involved police officers. Needless to say, my hatred for the system—and those who worked in it—intensified.

Because of such experiences, my first encounter with the teachings in the Sermon on the Mount was troublesome. I wanted to bully the bully, torment the tormentor, and see the jailers jailed. However, the teaching of Jesus presented an apparently illogical response that—on the surface—appeared to vindicate the one who bore obvious guilt. For the remainder of this chapter we will try to make sense of what He has to say in one particular section of that sermon.

Upholding the Law

Jesus delivered the Sermon on the Mount shortly after He started His public ministry. Apparently it was not a general sermon for the multitudes that had already started flocking to Him, but an orientation of sorts to His inner core of disciples (see Matt. 5:1). Although often referred to as a sermon, we could probably more accurately describe it as a training lecture.

The text emphasizes that Jesus "sat down"—the normal posture of rabbis when they instructed their disciples.

The lecture is one of two lengthy presentations that Jesus shared with His inner circle, the other being the farewell discourse He delivered after they had consumed their final Passover meal together (see John 14:1-17:26). Occupying three chapters in Matthew's Gospel, the Sermon on the Mount has four distinct sections. Probably the most recognizable by name are the Beatitudes (Matt. 5:1-12). The briefest one, featuring metaphors of salt and light, has become known as the Similitudes (verses 13-16). Next comes the portion that many theologians call the Antithesis (verses 27-48). And the longest section contains the "ten commandments" of Christian behavior termed the Imperatives (Matt. 6:1-7:23). The lecture itself concludes with a call to action as Jesus shares a parable emphasizing the necessity of a spiritually firm foundation (verses 24-27).

The Antithesis is the section of the Sermon on the Mount that most directly relates to our study on the New Testament teaching on law. Personally, I'm not very fond of the term that theologians have chosen for it. Antithesis suggests that Jesus is countering a well-articulated "thesis," which some scholars believe was originally intended to indicate the Mosaic law. However, as a number of commentators recognize, "the term *antitheses* is something of a misnomer, for it can hardly be claimed that in all six paragraphs the teaching of Jesus is intended to be in direct contrast to, or opposition to (i.e., is "antithetical" to), the Law of Moses."[1] In fact, from the very outset of this section, Jesus is crystal clear that it was never His intention to abolish "the law or the prophets" (Matt. 5:17), which would have included the law of Moses.

The formulaic expression "law and prophets" appears several times in the New Testament and more than likely refers to the entire Old Testament canon.[2] By placing the Mosaic law in its literary context, Jesus is affirming what Paul would later state when he declared that *all* Scripture is divinely inspired (2 Tim. 3:16). True citizens of the kingdom do not have the authority to choose which parts of the Bible they will accept as authoritative. If God's Word is contained in "the law or the prophets," then all who claim to follow Him have a responsibility to obey all Scripture.

As Jesus explains later in His orientation lecture, those who submit to God's Word must know how to apply its teachings in a responsible fashion. On some level or the other, every person who accepts the authority of Scripture needs to embrace basic instructions for biblical interpretation. At the elementary level, Bible students should know that some passages of the

Bible are *descriptive* and others are *prescriptive*. In other words, some passages *describe* what happened in a narrative set in a certain place or time. They are not meant to be taken as instructions for all people at all times. Adversely, in other texts the Holy Spirit through the author *prescribes* a pattern of behavior that all believers are expected to follow. *Prescriptive* texts are not bound by time or culture.

When taken to another level of biblical interpretation, Bible students also recognize that we can find some timeless *prescriptions*/principles in *descriptive* passages of Scripture. For instance, a significant portion of the first five books of the Bible contains laws given to Israel. Some of them refer to issues surrounding Temple sacrifice and various cultural taboos. Then others not only identify sinful behavior but detail the punishment that should accompany that behavior.

When interpreting such laws, we should not forget that God gave them in a specific religious and political context in which Israel existed as a theocratic nation and had the authority to execute penalties on those who violated the legal code. We cannot ignore this reality when applying Scripture to our twenty-first-century context. For instance, divinity still deems it morally unacceptable for children to disrespect their parents or for a human to engage in sexual intercourse with an animal. Nonetheless, since the *penalties* described were entrusted to a distinct geopolitical body of people known as the Israelites who were a part of a unique covenant with God, they do not apply to our specific contemporary context.

Fully aware that in just a few decades after His death the Jewish nation will cease to exist, Jesus is careful to stress the enduring authority of God's Word. The many modern Christians who teach that the legal prescriptions of the Old Testament are no longer relevant need to hear Jesus anew: "I have come not to abolish but to fulfill" (Matt. 5:17). Jesus states His purpose as one in which He provides the proper meaning of God's Word as He reveals to people the supernatural power behind the pages. More specifically, as it relates to the law He teaches, "For truly I tell you, until heaven and earth pass away, not one letter, not one stroke of a letter, will pass from the law until all is accomplished" (verse 18). Jesus makes it clear that God's law is binding until the moment time merges into eternity.

So important is fidelity to His law that He warns His disciples: "Therefore, whoever breaks one of the least of these commandments, and teaches others to do the same, will be called least in the kingdom of heaven; but whoever does them and teaches them will be called great in the kingdom of heaven" (verse 19). At first glance it seems as if Jesus promotes a two-tiered heaven in which the lawbreakers are last in line and the law doers are first. Realistically it is a reminder that the spirit of lawless rebellion that incites people to licentious recklessness will result in many professed Christians being barred from the kingdom. God seeks children who are so serious about their covenant with Him that they are willing to have Him guide their thoughts and actions. As we saw in the previous chapter, they possess the righteousness missing from the motives of the Pharisees and scribes.

Murder and Marriage

Thankfully, Jesus did not speak just in abstract terms—He took the time to illustrate His teaching. He wanted His disciples to understand in practical ways what it meant to have righteousness that exceeded that of the Pharisees. His first example is shocking. Invoking the sixth commandment, He recited, "You have heard that it was said to those of ancient times, 'You shall not murder'; and 'whoever murders shall be liable to judgment'" (verse 21).[3] For the most part, the disciples could join the scribes and Pharisees in checking it off their list. They had not killed anyone with premeditated malice. However, the Spirit-filled Rabbi was not finished: "But I say to you that if you are angry with a brother or sister, you will be liable to judgment; and if you insult a brother or sister, you will be liable to the council; and if you say, 'You fool,' you will be liable to the hell of fire" (verse 22).

All of a sudden the disciples probably felt like those who accused the woman caught in the act of adultery. None of them may have physically taken a life, but at some time in their existence they had all been guilty of harboring hate, throwing insults, or cursing somebody out. The mirror had turned toward them, and the image reflected in it was not pretty at all. Jesus' lesson was very simple: the act of murder is merely the physical manifestation of a destructive spirit that has possessed most if not all of us in varying degrees. That painful emotion that steels the heart and conjures internal feelings of disdain and hate toward another is the very fuel that pushes some to the point of taking a person's life. Here is Jesus' point: the mere fact that one possesses the will to murder makes them a murderer—the act begins with a thought.

Fortunately for the disciples, even as they wrestled with their guilt, Jesus provided a remedy for them: "So when you are offering your gift at the altar, if you remember that your brother or sister has something against you, leave your gift there before the altar and go; first be reconciled to your brother or sister, and then come and offer your gift" (verses 23, 24). Children of the kingdom should be proactive agents of peace and reconciliation. The scenario that Jesus depicts is one in which the worshipper is the offender. Perhaps the worshipper is offering the gift on the altar with the belief that the sacrifice would cover their offense. However, such an act of outer righteousness is not enough to evoke God's forgiveness. Any legalistic scribe or Pharisee could easily go through the motions of sacrifice while harboring contempt toward another.

In order to experience the level of righteousness that Jesus demands, the believer must adopt a spirit of humility and approach the hurting person with the purpose of mending the relationship. In a very real way it will lead to a double miracle of grace, since the person "who has something against" the offender is also given the opportunity to release themselves from the desire for vengeance. They have the opportunity to live out the line in the Lord's Prayer that states, "Forgive us our debts as we forgive our debtors."[4] When such inner righteousness manifests itself, it rescues two individuals from the grip of the evil one.

Having explained the "spirit" behind the prohibition against murder, Jesus changes the topic to marital fidelity. His pattern of instruction is the same: "You have heard that it was said, 'You shall not commit adultery'" (verse 27). Given the frequency of adultery, I wouldn't be surprised if a couple of disciples suddenly felt as if a spotlight had targeted them, while others felt smug in their influence. However, Jesus was not yet finished: "But I say to you that everyone who looks at a woman with lust has already committed adultery with her in his heart" (verse 28).

Once more the disciples found themselves forced to take an inventory of their thoughts. They may not have engaged in illicit sexual relations with another man's wife. Nevertheless, they could recall the time when the smell of that woman's perfume invited them to take a second prolonged look. Probably they could even remember with vivid accuracy the alluring magnetism of her veil-framed eyes that incited a multiseries fantasy in their creative minds. Undoubtedly the principle behind Jesus' explanation goes beyond the realm of marriage to all categories of sexual sin.

Jesus' solution to this frequent human dilemma sounds atrociously extreme: "If your right eye causes you to sin, tear it out and throw it away. . . . And if your right hand causes you to sin, cut it off and throw it away; it is better for you to lose one of your members than for your whole body to go into hell" (verses 29, 30). Fortunately not too many people during the course of history have taken the text as an invitation to self-amputation. In fact, nowhere in the Gospels do we read of anyone employing such sadistically drastic measures to secure a place in God's kingdom.

Jesus is intentionally hyperbolic at this point because He wants to impress upon His disciples the need for disciplined self-control. It is a lesson often forgotten by those who misunderstand the true meaning of grace. I have heard many a person reason that if God did not want them to practice a certain sin, He would never have made them that way. However, the Bible provides another picture of an empowering grace that aids people to do the right thing (cf. Titus 2:11, 12). The radical eye extraction that Jesus requires involves the removal of external objects that serve as stimuli for sexual fantasies.[5]

Fully aware that lustful thoughts can overcome even a person without physical sight, the call to pluck out an eye is a summons to stop illicit thoughts in their tracks by focusing on things spiritual (see Phil. 4:8). The same is true for the recommended hand amputation. The reference to the hand implies action, often preceded or accompanied by sight. However, this example teaches that thoughts do not have to be followed up by action. Resisting sexual temptation may be as difficult as making the decision to remove one of your own body parts, but those with spiritual resolve will know that they can do all things through the One who empowers (see verse 13). It is in leaning on His transforming grace that the disciple experiences the righteousness that "exceeds that of the scribes and Pharisees" (Matt. 5:20).

Such righteousness will also encourage godly couples to stay together in marriage. Jesus is well aware that many people viewed the Mosaic allowance for divorce as a commandment, and rather than putting in the effort to build happy relationships they sought for excuses to exit the marriage on "biblical grounds." He minces no words with His admonition: "It was also said, 'Whoever divorces his wife, let him give her a certificate of divorce'" (verse 31). The disciples would have been aware that grounds for divorce were so loose that some rabbis even allowed it if the husband no longer found his wife attractive![6] Jesus put a new lock on that faulty back door with His qualifier: "But I say to you that anyone who divorces his wife, except on the ground of unchastity, causes her to commit adultery; and whoever marries a divorced woman commits adultery" (verse 32).

Jesus is crystal clear that God-centered marriages are intended to last for a lifetime. In fact, the very ground He provides for a "legitimate" divorce suggests that what He really had in mind was an annulment of a marriage in which it was found that the wife had engaged in *premarital* sex with another man.[7] His admonition also makes the husband responsible for his ex-wife's adultery, which is the sin she would commit if she married another man. The issue is further complicated by Jesus' declaration that any man who marries a divorced woman is also guilty of adultery—since in His estimation, she is still married to the first husband. Rather than providing further loopholes and/or escape clauses for those seeking to get out of a marriage, Jesus is basically encouraging those who are serious about possessing righteousness to do all they can to create a happy life together.

Vows and Vengeance

It is probably no coincidence that after His talk on the permanence of marriage, Jesus transitions into a discussion about vows. Assuming His disciple's Bible knowledge, He recounts: "Again, you have heard that it was said to those of ancient times, 'You shall not swear falsely, but carry out the vows you have made to the Lord'" (verse 33). Here, He actually alludes to two commandments from the Mosaic code. The first comes from a cluster that addresses dishonest behavior: "You shall not steal; you shall not deal falsely; and you shall not lie to one another. And *you shall not swear falsely by my name, profaning the name of your God: I am the Lord*" (Lev. 19:11, 12). The second He draws from Deuteronomy: "*If you make a vow to the Lord your God, do not postpone fulfilling it; for the Lord your God will surely require it of you, and you would incur guilt*" (Deut. 23:21).

It does not seem difficult to understand the ideal promoted in these passages. God is simply calling people to be true to their word. However, some among the rabbis had complicated the issue by establishing rules regulating precise formulas for making vows. Eventually, they got so caught up in dissecting legalistic minutia that the original purpose of the laws became buried in confusion. As we see in Jesus' extended rebuke of the scribes and Pharisees, competing schools of interpreters challenged even each other on what holy object they could use to establish a vow (see Matt. 23:18). It's in this context that we are to understand Jesus' explanation of the deeper meaning of the law: "But I say to you, Do not swear at all, either by heaven, for it is the throne of God, or by the earth, for it is his footstool, or by Jerusalem, for it is the city of the great King. And do not swear by your head, for you cannot make one hair white or black" (Matt. 5:34-36).

Those possessing the righteousness Jesus calls for do not need to establish their honesty with superstitious words. Invoking the witness of things sacred or profane in no way guarantees that anybody will do what they say.

Unlike the target of the original injunction, citizens of Christ's kingdom have no intent to defraud one another and see no need to make boastful public announcements about their monetary pledges to God. They understand that moral credibility does not manifest merely in words, but proves itself only at the point of action. Hence Jesus' final word on the topic: "Let your word be 'Yes, Yes' or 'No, No'; anything more than this comes from the evil one" (verse 37).

The discussion on vows skillfully leads into the next topic. The society into which Jesus entered our world was one based on the ethics of honor and shame. A large part of maintaining honor involved responding to a perpetrator with equal or greater force after being shamed. In such a culture revenge was not an option—it was an obligation! It is in this setting that Jesus pulls from another Mosaic commandment: "You have heard that it was said, 'An eye for an eye and a tooth for a tooth'" (verse 38; cf. Ex. 21:23, 24). The disciples would have immediately recognized it as a foundational law of practically all societies until that time, one best known today by the Latin term *lex talionis*, which literally means "law of retaliation." For many, it was the societal version of Sir Isaac Newton's third law of motion (for every action there is an equal and opposite reaction).

Once again the disciples must have readied themselves for deconstruction. Jesus doesn't disappoint as He provides a rejoinder to the seemingly ubiquitous law: "But I say to you, Do not resist an evildoer. But if anyone strikes you on the right cheek, turn the other also; and if anyone wants to sue you and take your coat, give your cloak as well; and if anyone forces you to go one mile, go also the second mile" (Matt. 5:39-41). It must have sounded nonsensical to His disciples. What would they have to gain by allowing people to abuse and take advantage of them? However, as Martin Luther King, Jr., recognized, Jesus' call to nonviolent resistance is a very effective way of engaging an enemy.

The act of turning the other cheek is not an invitation for further abuse, but a signal to the evildoer that the offended person refuses to respond in kind. It indicates a willingness to enter into a truce with one whose violent action gave the victim every right to avenge themselves. Likewise, preemptively offering one's *cloak* to a person who wants to sue them for their *coat* indicates a desire to settle the dispute without malice. Further, going an extra mile when impressed by a Roman soldier to carry his load for one mile demonstrates a willingness to relieve another person of humiliation. The decision to withhold retaliation not only provides a lesson on kindness, but also places the victims in control. In addition to choosing to be kind to their offender, their honorable behavior transfers the shame to the one who has tried to dishonor them!

The theme of proactive engagement is also present in the final antithesis. Here, Jesus refers to a common sentiment that has no direct parallel in biblical law: "You have heard that it was said, 'You shall love your neighbor and hate your enemy'" (verse 43). Although it has no biblical precedent, it was probably the law *du jour* for a people living under Roman occupation. However, Jesus would once again upset the status quo with His admonition, "But I say to you, Love your enemies and pray for those who persecute you" (verse 44). Although probably the hardest saying of all, it was yet the one most illustrative of the righteousness to which Jesus called them—a righteousness grounded in God.

As He closes this segment of the sermon, Jesus presents the real reason for His spiritual teaching: "So that you may be children of your Father in heaven; for he makes the sun rise on the evil and on the good, and sends rain on the righteous and on the unrighteous" (verse 45). God's goodness is not selective. He loves even those who hate Him and question His existence. Here is the love to which He calls His disciples—the same love that fills the essence of His law. It is in this light that we understand His final command in this section: "Be perfect, therefore, as your heavenly Father is perfect" (verse 48).

Conclusion

We see the path to spiritual perfection wonderfully demonstrated in the so-called Antitheses. Rather than being an abrogation of divine laws that came before it, this part of the Sermon on the Mount is a corrective to the legalists who had manipulated the law and transformed it into an object of slavery. Jesus is clear that He has no intention of doing away with His Father's perfect law that so eloquently expresses His perfect will.

Each antithesis unveils an aspect of the perfect behavior that will exude from those who possess the righteousness that exceeds that of the Pharisees. Refusing to intentionally hurt others, they will seek harmony in their relationships. Instead of being possessed with lustful thoughts, they will intentionally build marriages in which love is truly the ruling factor. They will not attempt to deceive or impress people with empty promises, but will strive to be honest in their dealings. Nor will they seek revenge when someone has challenged their honor. Rather, they will act honorably to all people—even those who would seek to cause them shame. And finally, they will not show hatred to those who are "different" or appear to deserve it, but will treat them with kindness and consideration.

Soon after I finished high school, a friend informed me that he had spotted my former woodwork teacher on the high street. Just the mention of his name made my blood boil. My deep-seated desire for revenge overwhelmed me so much that I was almost oblivious to the rest of the story. Apparently my abusive teacher was no longer the robust man he had once been. Alcohol had consumed him, and he roamed the streets like a vagrant without a purpose. The news of his early demise brought me temporary joy. However, years later the Spirit reminded me that all of us have sinned and lack God's glory. We had both been in need of saving grace, and my responsibility would have been to pray for him with the same passion with which he had preyed on me.

Recently I had the privilege to engage T. Marshall Kelly in conversation. I always feel honored to sit at the feet of this great man of God whose humility is both genuine and legendary. He shared his experience of encountering overt racism as he matriculated through one of our schools several decades ago. His way of dealing with it was embracing Romans 12:21 as his life mission statement: "Do not be overcome by evil, but overcome evil with good." By imbibing the principles laid out in the Sermon on the Mount, he witnessed the transforming power of God's love as many of those who hated him eventually embraced him. I have no doubt that all who truly delight in God's law will share Kelly's experience.

---

[1] G. N. Stanton, "Sermon on the Mount/Plain," in J. B. Green, S. McKnight, and I. H. Marshall, eds., *Dictionary of Jesus and the Gospels* (Downers Grove, Ill.: InterVarsity Press, 1992), p. 742.

[2] It is not exactly clear at what point in history people began to use the tripartite designation: law, prophets, and writings.

[3] For reasons unexplained, the translators of the King James Version rendered the commandment, "Thou shalt not kill." However, the Hebrew reads, "Thou shalt not murder." Although often seen as synonyms, the difference between the two is premeditation.

[4] For a person who withholds forgiveness, the phrase is actually a curse on one's self!

[5] In his comment on this passage W. W. Wiersbe, in *The Bible Exposition Commentary* (Wheaton, Ill.: Victor Books. 1996), states, "Of course, He did not command us to perform *physical* surgery, since He was clearly dealing with the *inner* desires. He commanded us to deal drastically with sin, to remove from our lives anything that would pamper our wrong desires."

[6] See Keith Augustus Burton, "A Christian Theology of Divorce and Remarriage," *Ministry*, April 2001, pp. 20-22.

[7] *Ibid.*

CHAPTER 5

Christ and the Sabbath Law

During my recent conversations with T. Marshall Kelly we discussed the exemplary fidelity of Andrews University professor Miroslav Kis. Born in Communist Yugoslavia, Kis became convinced about the Sabbath at the age of 8 and suffered terrible physical abuse at the hand of a teacher when he refused to attend classes on *subota*. God was able to deliver him from his spiteful persecutor, but it would not be the only occasion that his fidelity to God caused him hardship. In his 20s while serving in the Yugoslav military, he had to choose between working on the Sabbath and being court-martialed. Once more he witnessed the hand of God operating in his life.

Heroes such as Kis fascinated me as a youngster when I listened to mission stories in Sabbath school. I admired those young stalwarts and wished so much that I could be like them, but I wasn't. My experience with Sabbath was quite different. The truth is, I was anything *but* a proud Sabbath observer. The England in which I was raised was a severely secular country, and few people attended church on Sundays, much less on Sabbaths. Paranoia filled my weekly Sabbath treks from my family home to the bus stop at Norwood Junction. I lagged behind my parents to make it seem as if I were by myself, and tried my best to hide my bulging Bible. If I saw someone I knew, I would avert my head to disguise my identity and avoid making eye contact.

High school days were even more challenging. Sports were out of the question, since the major games were on Sabbaths, and I found myself constantly inventing new excuses for not attending the many social events my classmates enjoyed on God's day of rest. I still recall the day three members of my trusty crew located my home just as I had finished Sabbath dinner and invited me to accompany them to the movies. As I dug into my mind for an excuse, one of them inquired why I was dressed in a shirt and tie. It provided me with an opportunity to blurt out the first lie that entered my mind: "I had to go to a wedding!" Apparently it worked, because my friends politely apologized for disturbing the celebrations and made a quick exit. After several other chance encounters with schoolmates on Sabbaths, one eventually commented, "You sure get invited to a lot of weddings!"

Just in case you are wondering, my embarrassment about Sabbath observance had little to do with my parents. Mom and Dad went out of their way to create an environment in which Sabbath felt special for the 12 of us who inhabited our three-bedroom home (for most of those years the reception room served as a fourth bedroom). We completed most of the housework on Thursday evening. It was also the time we inspected our Sabbath clothes and polished all shoes to a mirror shine. On Fridays, before we even entered the front door, the smell of baked treats filled the entire perimeter of our home. In addition to the several loaves of whole-wheat bread and scrumptious oversized dinner rolls, Dad would always make his famous crispy-topped cake and a Jamaican soft-topped cornmeal pudding or a coconut *toto*.

After a delightful Sabbath evening meal, we would retire to the tiny living room, where we engaged in rousing singing; always accompanied by piano and at times acoustic guitar, bass guitar, trumpet, or even the occasional drum set. The euphoria from the song service made the 12-person session of prayer a little more bearable (it wasn't easy kneeling for 15 minutes!). We then transitioned into testimonies and recital of our "memorized" memory verses before reviewing our lesson studies. Once worship ended, we made the short trip back to the dining room, where we were treated to a generous slice of one of the sweet treats Dad had baked, accompanied by some hot or cold sweetened beverage. In spite of my embarrassment while walking to the bus stop the following Sabbath morning, on Friday (Sabbath) evenings I always went to bed with a smile.

After morning church activities, we would make our way home, where we often had guests. Sabbath afternoon meal was doubly special and almost always included my mother's famous macaroni-and-cheese recipe, complete with a rissole nut crust. The dessert was extra-special, and we savored every mouthwatering morsel of Dad's baked treats, homemade fruit salads, and ice cream. Sometimes in the summer my parents would announce that we would be eating our Sabbath meal at Shirley Woods' house. I loved these impromptu picnics. On those days the children consumed their food rather rapidly and received permission to explore the natural surroundings (but only after being warned to keep in parental view!).

As I reflect on my childhood Sabbath memories, I have to admit that in spite of my public embarrassment, I privately learned what it meant to experience what our Jewish friends refer to as *oneg Shabbat*—the joy of the Sabbath. As I matured in Christ (and in chronology), I began to appreciate the Sabbath even more. This delightful day has proven to be a temporal oasis that offers me refreshment from a chaos-filled week of meetings, study, research, DIY projects, deadlines, and a host of other *things* that contribute to life's busyness. For the rest of this chapter, we will discover how the Sabbath is *one of* the most precious gifts that God has given to humans.

The Sabbath Command

The original meaning of some words is so obvious that they shouldn't really need to be explained. However, in some instances the meanings have become muddled over time. For instance, the expression *baptism by immersion* is actually a redundancy, since "baptism" *is* immersion. Those who first used the word *baptisma* for this important Christian ritual chose it because it meant to them what "immersion" means to us. Another example of the weakening of a word's original significance appears in "Jewish Sabbath" or "Christian Sabbath." I am fully aware that people automatically think "Saturday" and "Sunday" when they decode the terms, but for its original hearers the word "Sabbath" did not need qualifying. While it is true that Scripture does have passages that used "Sabbath" adjectivally as a synonym for "holy day" (as in the case of Yom Kippur or Passover), the fact that the term itself derived from the word for "seven" should be enough to establish the primary connotation.

In spite of the original meaning of "Sabbath," centuries of programmed propaganda have effectively brainwashed billions of professed Christians into believing that God has changed His mind about the day He originally declared holy. On any given weekend the majority of people who attend a place of worship do so on a Sunday. So ubiquitous is the practice that the majority of Christians often view the few denominations that maintain fidelity to the biblical Sabbath as legalists, Judaizers, nontraditionalists, or cultic. Nonetheless, such disdain cannot change an immutable and undisputable truth: the Sabbath *is* and *always has been* the seventh day of the week.[1]

During the past 20 centuries not all Christians have been willing to abandon the Sabbath in favor of a pagan day to honor the sun. The truth is, it was only natural for the earliest believers to continue the biblically grounded practice they had inherited from their Jewish forebears. In fact, even as a growing number of Christians allowed the day of the sun to eclipse that of the Son, there has always existed a faithful remnant who have rhythmically ceased from their labors on the day that God made.[2] One of the strongest testimonies appears in the witness of the Ethiopian *Tewahedo* church, which has championed Sabbath observance since its founding in the fourth century.[3] Interestingly, a number of tribes that share Ethiopia's continent have also echoed the Sabbath call, even if they do not self-identify as Jews or Christians.[4]

The stubborn persistence of Sabbath observance in a world that elevates Sunday is evidence that God is still in control. Bishops and politicians may succeed in influencing calendar makers to list Monday as the first day of the week, but the faithful will always bear witness to the unchanging God. They understand that Yahweh's selection of the seventh day was by no means arbitrary. God did not intend the choice of day to be an adjustable principle that one could apply to any of the days that comprise the week. Sabbath is a unique and incomparable day—the only one that God blessed and sanctified (Gen. 2:3).

The mere fact that He blessed and consecrated a *day* gives reason for pause. Blessing and consecration are holy acts usually performed on tangible objects—whether animate or inanimate. However, a *day* is unlike a physical temple or firstborn son. It cannot be felt, heard, tasted, seen, or smelled. Yet God has endowed it with a perpetual blessing. The act itself is both mystifying and mysterious as we contemplate the unfathomable wisdom of an omniscient God who has constructed an invisible tabernacle in time. In some mystical way, the Sabbath stands as a testament of a Deity so immense that He can never be fully seen but can always be existentially experienced. On this *day* all humans receive an opportunity to immerse themselves in the divine as they share the blessings and impact of the holiness contained therein.

Although an explicit biblical command to observe the Sabbath does not appear until the account of the giving of the Ten Commandments, scholars have long recognized the implications of the words in Genesis 2: 1-3. A popular commentary by renowned evangelical scholars states, "Here, God is described as resting on the seventh day, but the narrator clearly implies that mankind, made in the divine image, is expected to copy his Creator. Indeed, the context implies that a weekly day of rest is as necessary for human survival as sex (Gen. 1:27, 28) or food (1:29)."[5] Unfortunately, while a number of non-Sabbathkeeping scholars interpret the text as a divine command, they read it in a way that obfuscates the exact day of rest. For instance, in the previous quote, by referring in general terms to "a weekly day of rest" the commentators ingenuously assert that the actual day on which one rests does not matter.

Reading the Exodus account of the fourth commandment will quickly quash any notion that God's day of rest is based on individual subjective determination. It clearly indicates *what* day He has in mind: "Remember the sabbath day, and keep it holy. *Six days* you shall labor and do all your work. But the seventh day is [the] sabbath to the Lord your God" (Ex. 20:8-10). In no uncertain terms Scripture sets the day on which Sabbath falls in the context of the divinely ordained week. Just in case anybody chose to be contentious about the exact parameters of the week, God gives the rationale for Sabbath observance: "For in six days the Lord made the heaven and earth, the sea, and all that is in them, but rested the seventh day; therefore the Lord blessed the sabbath day and consecrated it" (verse 11).

Not only is it important for those who submit to the authority of the Bible to know that God appointed a specific day, but it is also necessary to understand the meaning of "rest." The Bible is clear that after six days of activity God stopped creating and "rested." In our mortal understanding, an individual needs rest because they are tired and need to be rejuvenated. However, does the God of all creation who speaks universes into existence get weary? Was the construction of our solar system so exhausting that He had to take a nap? Of course not! The omnipotent God, who neither sleeps nor slumbers, intentionally refrained from creative activity for that 24-hour period because He wanted to fill it with blessings and holiness. The Sabbath is as much a part of His creation as all the tangible things that He called into existence on the first six days.

When a person chooses to cease from daily activities on the Sabbath, they demonstrate their faith in the God who has made both the visible and invisible. Although such an act of faith has physical benefits, its ultimate objective is spiritual. Humans turn away from their typical daily routines on the Sabbath because they want to experience their Creator in a way that is just not possible on any other day. The spirit-filled intermission seeks to remind all who benefit from it that the all-powerful God is not distantly removed from His creation—He is ever present. On the Sabbath we experience the God who loves us so much that He has set up a recurring appointment with us in His eternal calendar.

Freedom and the Sabbath

For our post-sin world, the Sabbath is also a symbol of God's prevailing grace. The Exodus account of the fourth commandment reminds us to observe the Sabbath in honor of Him as Creator. However, the rationale in the Deuteronomy version is radically different: "Remember that you were a slave in the land of Egypt, and the Lord your God brought you out from there with a mighty hand and outstretched arm; therefore the Lord your God commanded you to keep the sabbath day" (Deut. 5:15). Addressing the newly emancipated slaves, Moses here points to the true potency of the Sabbath.

After decades of abuse and dehumanizing treatment, a massive loss of confidence had crippled the Israelites. They were used to the humiliation of bowing before their cruel masters. Their collective esteem had slowly dissipated as shame consumed them. But not all was lost for a disheartened people whom God had called for greatness. They could transcend their sense of worthlessness by looking to the Lord who had rescued them from their deplorable condition. Indeed, it is this same God who invited them to reclaim their real identity by observing His Sabbath. It was not a command that banished them to slavish legalism, but an invitation to emancipation from oppressive human hierarchies. Keeping the Sabbath immediately elevated their status as they experienced a mystical union with a God who infused the day with His own holiness!

Similar to the command in Exodus that requests Sabbath observance from all of God's creation and not just the Israelites, Deuteronomy is careful to enumerate those who should benefit from Sabbath rest: "You, . . . your son, . . . your daughter, . . . your male [and] female slave, . . . your ox, . . . your donkey, . . . any of your livestock, [and] the resident alien in your towns, so that your male and female slave may rest as well as you" (verse 14). The God of all nations is not partial. The Israelite has no more claim to the blessings of God's Sabbath than the Egyptian, Canaanite, Hittite, or Canadian. The Jew has no more claim on the Sabbath than the Christian, Rastafarian, Muslim, or Taoist. On this glorious day all of God's creation has an opportunity to reflect on the One who has liberated every one of us from the slavery of sin.

Ironically, too many people miss the real meaning of Sabbath and view it as a day of bondage rather than liberation. We see this all too clear in the attitude of the Pharisees who chastised Jesus' disciples for plucking grain on the Sabbath to satisfy their hunger (Mark 2:23-28). As mentioned in a previous chapter, the Pharisees' intent on keeping the commandments had led them to create countless other minor laws. Thirty-nine laws surrounded the Sabbath commandment alone, and each one was subject to any number of interpretations that in themselves gained the force of law. When the Pharisees spotted the disciples plucking grain as they leisurely walked, all their legalistic minds could see was heavy farming equipment in full operation during the harvest! They were so removed from the law of love that they now possessed a paranoia that had them permanently imprisoned.

Probably overcome by pity for their pious fear, Jesus quickly corrected the Pharisees as He took the opportunity to open their eyes to the grace embedded in God's Word. Appealing to their scriptural knowledge, He asked: "Have you never read what David did when he and his companions were hungry and in need of food? He entered the house of God, when Abiathar was high priest, and ate the bread of the Presence, which it is not lawful for any but the priests to eat, and he gave some to his companions" (verses 25, 26). It probably took a little time for the Pharisees to understand Jesus' point, since the Bible does not indicate that the incident to which Jesus referred occurred on the Sabbath (see 1 Sam. 21:1-6). However, Jesus employed it to elevate the God of grace and liberty who does not make laws to enslave us but to provide us with a more perfect reflection of His loving image.

After sharing the example of David's violation of a functional law, Jesus establishes His real point: "The sabbath was made for humankind, and not humankind for the sabbath" (Mark 2:27). Directing them to Genesis, He reminds the Pharisees that the Sabbath is a created institution—it is not the Creator. A vehicle for worship, it is not the object of worship. Instead, it is a day on which people take a break from routine activities classified under the category of work, not a day for people to withdraw from *all* activities. It is a day when God asks us to avoid our *own* pleasure, not a day when we refrain from seeking His pleasure. The Sabbath is God's perpetual gift to His creation—a day on which He constantly reminds us that our Creator desires unbridled communication with us. Like no other day, the Sabbath is a powerful symbol of God's love.

Healing and the Sabbath

Indeed, it is because of the unique symbolism packed into the Sabbath that Jesus went out of His way to perform healings during that sanctified time. Sickness is not a part of God's original order. This manifestation of the enemy's destructive power constantly reminds us that humans have lost the elevated status that God had bestowed on them at Creation. Although people can learn to function with their maladies, few will turn down the opportunity to have their situation reversed. That was especially true in Jesus' society, where there were no hearing aids, cataract surgeries, or high-tech prosthetic devices. People afflicted with debilitating illnesses basically had to accept them as their lot in life.

The four Sabbath healings recorded in the Gospels demonstrate Jesus' desire to reshape people's understanding of a day whose meaning had been lost in a gloomy sea of legalism.[6] For most, Sabbath was a burdensome day during which people were so occupied with their not-to-do checklists that they totally missed the blessings that God had reserved for them. Jesus knew that those who promoted such a legalistic approach to the Sabbath were in effect spreading lies about the nature of His Father. They were portraying a "god" who takes pleasure in people's misery. It wasn't the kind of deity that Jesus knew or came to reveal. The Pharisees' "sabbath" may have fallen on the seventh day of the week, but it was *not* the Sabbath of the loving Lord.

God's true Sabbath is not a day of bondage, but one of liberation. Jesus drives this point home when He healed the woman who had suffered from a spinal deformity for 18 years (Luke 13:10-17). When the leader of the synagogue objected to the healing, Jesus proclaimed, "Ought not this woman, a daughter of Abraham whom Satan bound for eighteen long years, be set free from this bondage on the sabbath day?" (Luke 13:16). As far as Jesus was concerned, alleviating suffering on the Sabbath was more important than submitting to human-made rules. In fact, He seemed to go out of His way to find long-term sufferers for Sabbath miracles. The paralytic at the Pool of Bethesda had been lame for 38 years (John 5:5), and the man who regained his sight after washing in the Pool of Siloam had been blind from birth (John 9:1). Both of them learned firsthand that the God of Creation can reverse decades—even millennia—of Satan's damage in a single moment.

Given the spectacular results of Jesus' Sabbath healing ministries, it is difficult to understand why they upset some religious leaders. Apparently they had become so enamored by the day itself that it obscured their view of the One who made the day. In fact, the Sabbath healing recorded in Mark 3:1-6 occurs soon after the aforementioned incident when the Pharisees chastised Jesus' disciples for plucking grain on the Sabbath. Those who were truly in tune with the Spirit of God would have understood the meaning of Jesus' pronouncement that God had created the Sabbath to benefit humanity. However, those miserable legalists hardened their ears and hearts to the voice of the Spirit, and "watched him to see whether he would cure him on the sabbath, so that they may accuse him" (verse 2).

Their hatred of Jesus had so blinded them that they did not even think through the implications of their entrapment. The commandment is clear that God has requested humans to refrain from secular work on the Sabbath, but how in the world does miraculous healing fall under the category of secular "work"? In their pious arrogance they wanted to put restrictions on God Himself! And in losing sight of the God of the Sabbath, they had failed to connect to the same God of love. Hence Jesus' attempt to drive the meaning of the Sabbath home with His question "Is it lawful to do good or to do harm on the sabbath, to save life or to kill?" (verse 4). The answer to His rhetorical question should have been obvious to true seekers of God's will, but Jesus' opponents refused to respond. Undeterred by their attempts to intimidate Him, Jesus—filled with righteous indignation—ordered the afflicted man to stretch out his hand, and with the healing came an even deeper determination by the Pharisees to destroy Him (verses 5, 6).

Ironically, many proponents of Sunday observance share the Pharisees' attitude toward Sabbath healing when they claim that Jesus' Sabbath miracles amount to a transgression of the law. However, unlike the Pharisees, who pressed for the prosecution of those *they* believed to be Sabbath "violators," Sunday observers encourage individuals to treat the day with impunity. As if overcome by a powerful intoxicant, they proudly denounce God's Sabbath as they embrace a day that has never received divine endorsement. Such a shift of allegiance makes no logical sense. We can attribute it only to the master of lies, who deceived our common foreparents in Eden.

Jesus Himself corrected the legalists' false understanding about Sabbath healing when He reminded them, "My Father is still working, and I also am working" (John 5:17). When professed Christians use the Sabbath healing miracles as justification to turn their back on God's Sabbath, they are in effect saying that the law of the Pharisees has more authority than the law of God. Their rejection of God's Sabbath also means that they themselves claim authority to replace God's laws with their own. While they claim "freedom," little do some Sunday observers know that they are in bondage to the same evil spirit that possessed the Pharisees.

Conclusion

God's Sabbath is neither temporary nor optional. He established it at Creation as a perpetual monument through which He and His creation could enjoy uninterrupted time together. On no other day did He infuse so much of His blessings and holiness. Of course, He is well aware that humans are free to worship Him on any day and at any time, but the Sabbath affords an opportunity for unbridled devotion. On this day there are no pressures of work and business. In a mysterious way time stands still and invites us into a dimension in which it temporarily pauses for eternity.

Those who erroneously believe that Christians are no longer obligated to observe the day will do well to take another look at the early Christian witnesses. Not only did Jesus forecast that believers would be keeping the Sabbath after His ascension (cf. Matt. 24:20), but in clear terms the letter to the Hebrews reminds us that the practice of Sabbathkeeping is still in effect for God's people (Heb. 4:9). Indeed, on this day we have an opportunity to withdraw from time, just as God did at the end of Creation week (cf. verses 4, 10). Because the Sabbath is an inseparable part of Creation, we should not be surprised that in His description of the renewed world, the prophet Isaiah reminds us, "From new moon to new moon, and from sabbath to sabbath, all flesh shall come worship before [the Lord]" (Isa. 66:23).

I recall Clifford Goldstein telling the story of the Friday evening he was walking through the Golders Green section of London and an Orthodox Jew called him to turn her light on because the sun had just set. As far as she was concerned, it was a sin to operate the light switch on the Sabbath, since it was the equivalent of lighting a fire for domestic purposes. A few years ago I was on an international trip at the outset of winter. After preaching two morning sermons at two separate churches, we went to another for lunch. The cooked food that we were served was very cold, and although it looked appealing it was difficult for me to eat it at that temperature. My host sensed my discomfort and lamented, "I wish we were at my house; I could put the food in the microwave, but we have only a stove in this church and are not supposed to operate it on Sabbaths." Later that day I asked him for the rationale behind prohibiting the warming of food on a conventional stove but allowing for it to be heated in a microwave oven. It did not take long for him to see that in many ways they were no different from the Orthodox Jew who asked Clifford Goldstein to activate her light switch.

God created the Sabbath with us in mind. It is not a day of bondage on which we tread so carefully that the appearance of our own shadow makes us skittish. Instead, it is a day of liberation, during which we are free to bask in the blessings and lavish in the love that makes the time so special. A day like no other, the Sabbath invites us to spend quality time with our Creator and Redeemer. Whatever our station in life, the Lord's special day reminds us that we all stand equal before Him. The exclusivists, antagonists, and legalists may try to hijack the day as they promote persuasive lies about its intent, but those who truly love the Lord will not be intimidated by their pompous attempt to hide God's law under their human-made rules. God's people know that His holy Sabbath is filled with joy and healing, and they *will* "rejoice and be glad in it" (Ps. 118:24).

---

[1] R. Jamieson, A. R. Fausset, and D. Brown, in *Commentary Critical and Explanatory on the Whole Bible* (Oak Harbor, Wash.: Logos Research Systems, Inc., 1997), state: "The institution of the Sabbath is as old as creation, giving rise to that weekly division of time which prevailed in the earliest ages."

[2] See Kenneth Strand, ed., *The Sabbath in Scripture and History* (Washington, D.C.: Review and Herald Pub. Assn., 1982), pp. 132-243.

[3] See discussion in Keith Augustus Burton, *The Blessing of Africa: The Bible and African Christianity* (Downers Grove, Ill: InterVarsity Press, 2007), pp. 186-195, and Bekele Heye, *The Sabbath in Ethiopia: An Exploration of Christian Roots* (Lincoln, Nebr.: Center for Creative Ministry, 2003).

[4] See Charles E. Bradford, *Sabbath Roots: The African Connection* (Silver Spring, Md.: General Conference Ministerial Association, 1999), and Kofi Owusu-Mensah, *Saturday God and Adventism in Ghana* (Frankfurt am Main: Verlag Peter Lang, 1993).

[5] "Genesis 2:1-3," in D. A. Carson, R. T. France, J. A. Motyer, and G. J. Wenham, eds., *New Bible Commentary: 21st Century Edition*, 4th ed. (Downers Grove, Ill.: InterVarsity Press, 1994), p. 61.

[6] The man with a withered hand (Mark 3:1-6), the woman who had been bent over for 18 years (Luke 13:10-17), the invalid man who had been lying by the Pool of Bethesda for 38 years (John 5:1-9), and the man born blind (John 9:1-14).

CHAPTER 6

Christ's Death and the Law

Money was scarce in our family of 12. Allowance—we called it "pocket money"—was out of the question. If we wanted to buy toys, magazines, or crafts, we had to find a way to make it happen. My brothers and I were always on the lookout for glass bottles that we could take back to the store for a refund, or other items of value that we could trade for cash at the junk shop. During the holiday season we would tune up our voices and go caroling—not necessarily to bring joy to the neighbors, but to accumulate enough funds to buy Christmas gifts for our parents and siblings.

Opportunities for earning opened up in our tween years, but Sabbath observance severely limited our options. For instance, paper routes demanded a seven-day commitment, and we could offer only six. My sister Vanessa managed to secure a paper route for the local weekly that was distributed only on Thursdays and graciously allowed us to help her for a percentage of her already-meager pay. Always the entrepreneur, my brother Peter decided that he needed to broaden his horizons, and managed to secure another job on a milk delivery vehicle. He was generous enough to share the job with me, and we alternated days. I still remember waking up at 4:30 a.m. on freezing cold and rainy mornings to meet the customized delivery vehicle at the corner of Portland and Apsley roads.

In my final year of high school the best-ever earning opportunity opened up for me. My best friend's mother worked in the janitorial department of an office building and recommended my name for an opening. The fact that I did not have to work on Friday evenings was the icing on the cake. On the first day of work I couldn't wait to finish school so I could grab a quick bite and report for duty. My job description was rather basic. I was responsible for cleaning all bathrooms on the 20 floors. My supervisor took the time to show me how to clean a bathroom so thoroughly that a person could eat off the floor!

I took pride in my job and had planned a perfect procedure for my routine. First I would scrub and disinfect the commodes and urinals, paying close attention to those sections on the inside and outside not visible to the naked eye. I would then take a soft cloth and buff the porcelain and steel fixtures to a mirror shine. The cleaning materials for the sinks were in another part of my cart, and I repeated the ritual, inspecting every faucet for water stains or fingerprints. After ensuring that the mirrors were streak-free, I would wipe down the doors and handles and check for any noticeable defect on the walls before emptying the trash. Then I would sweep the floor, taking the time to ease the dirt from every corner in the room. Finally, I would roll in my custom pail and thoroughly mop the floor from the back of the room to the exit door.

For my first couple weeks on the job my supervisor inspected my work on a daily basis and called my attention to little things I may have missed. After a while she expressed her confidence in me, and the inspections became infrequent. Impressed by my work, she soon opened up opportunities for me to make more money by cleaning venetian blinds in the offices or buffing the floor of the main entrance. I was proud to be numbered among her most dependable workers.

Everything was going great until I made some choices that would eventually cost me my job. A friend was in need of work, and on the basis of my recommendation the supervisor hired him on the spot. He worked in a part of the building that I had never entered. It was the section that included the game room. The first time I ventured into the game room I couldn't believe my eyes. In the very building in which I had labored for several months was a room temptingly equipped with snooker, bar football and table tennis tables, and a fee-free pinball machine!

Work wasn't the same after that day. I began to rush through my tasks so that I could take the elevator to the game room and challenge my friend to table tennis or pinball. Often when I got there, he was already on the pinball machine trying to beat his high score. The security guard started to wonder why our two-hour shift was taking four hours to complete—especially since he noticed me descending to the basement after only an hour of work. The supervisor, alerted, confronted me one evening with a long list of infractions and a final paycheck. My friend received his also.

I learned a valuable lesson from the experience. When I first started working, my supervisor continuously checked my work and took the time to train me in the fine art of cleaning (I honestly believe it is an art!). After I had demonstrated my ability to follow instructions, my supervisor did not feel as if she needed to micromanage me. I'm sure she caught a couple mistakes in her infrequent inspections, but she trusted me so much that she knew that they were probably genuine oversights and never even mentioned them. It was only when she began to see a newly developing pattern in my work that she made the painful decision to terminate my employment. She needed to know that the person who had the job would be faithful to duty even in her absence. For the rest of this chapter we will discover that even though we cannot see Him, Christ expects us to demonstrate our faithfulness to Him by abiding by the terms of His law.

Two Weddings and a Funeral

It is no secret that the majority of professed Christians believe that Christ's death released us from the obligation to observe God's ten-commandment law.[1] Many see evidence of this in the analogy that Paul uses in Romans 7:1-6. While much debate exists about how to interpret the constituent parts of the analogy,[2] some scholars conclude that Paul wants to show the death of the law. However, when the text is analyzed in its various contexts, it is clear that Paul is saying the exact opposite. This analogy—like those that precede and follow it—actually heralds the abiding perpetuity of God's law.

In order for us to understand the passage, it is important to know the basics of how an analogy operates. In simple terms, it is a type of argument that uses a familiar concept to introduce an unfamiliar one—it has the same function as a parable. A well-developed analogical argument contains a premise, an illustration, and an application. The *premise* establishes the key to interpretation so that the listener does not have to guess the intended meaning. The *illustration* introduces a concept familiar to the listener, and the *application* (which is sometimes so obvious that it does not need stating) makes the link to an unfamiliar concept.

The premise of the analogy we are looking at appears in the first verse. I am well aware that several translations indicate or imply that the verse says "Death releases a person from the law." However, a literal translation from the original Greek reads: "The law rules over a person for as long as he is alive." Paul does not specifically mention death. Consequently, the premise is best stated as "Every living person is governed by law."[3]

The illustration section of the analogy introduces the familiar concept of marriage. The main character employed here is a married woman who "is bound by the law to her husband as long as he lives" (verse 2). As it pertains to the law of marriage, Paul reminds his audience, "Accordingly, she will be called an adulteress if she lives with another man while her husband is alive" (verse 3). From this statement it is clear that Paul has the ten-commandment prohibition against adultery in mind. As far as he is concerned, it is only the husband's death that can release the woman from the part of the law pertaining to her marriage. Notice that the law itself does not disappear, but the change in the woman's circumstance nullifies the applicability of that particular section of the law for her.

From the way that people frequently interpret the analogy, it appears as if they stop their analysis of the text at the point when Paul says that "if her husband dies, she is free from the law" (verse 3). However, key to understanding the argument is the clause that follows: "If she marries another man, she is not an adulteress" (verse 3). Remember, the premise of the argument is "every living person is governed by law." Consequently, while the death of her husband frees her to marry a new one, once the woman enters into a new marriage she is once again governed by the law—her status demands it! By now, it should be evident that many people misinterpret the text, because they automatically assume that the law in the illustration represents the husband.[4] However, it is clear that is not what Paul intended. The problem with the marriage was not the law, but the spouse. Here is the most important thing to remember as we examine the application section of the analogy.

Part of the confusion people face when interpreting the analogy stems from the following statement: "In the same way, my friends, you have died to the law through the body of Christ" (verse 4). It seems as if the illustration calls for the believer to identify with the wife, but here Paul states that the believer has died, which suggests that the husband is the correspondent. While this may at first seem confusing, it does clarify the fact that since the husband represents the believer he cannot symbolize the death of the law. Instead, the analogy demands that the believer identifies with both the wife *and* the husband.[5] Think of the wife as a person's "neutral" self and the husband as the "spiritual" self. In the first relationship, the husband represents sin. It is sin, not law, that poses a problem for humans. In order to release us from its power, Christ *became* sin and enabled our sinful self to die with Him (verse 4). With the death of our sinful self, the neutral self is now free to enter into another marriage relationship, this time with the resurrected Christ, who is the symbol of grace and righteousness.

Since the new relationship involves the living, the law is as applicable in the second relationship as it was in the first. However, the change in spouses makes all the difference. Listen to what Paul says about the first marriage: "While we were living in the flesh, our sinful passions . . . were at work in our members to bear fruit for death" (verse 5).[6] Someone trapped in the flesh has no choice but to view the law negatively, since it is a daily reminder of death. When seen in the light of the first husband, it is no wonder that Paul speaks of it as an "old written code" that "held us captive" (verse 6). On the contrary, the second marriage is one in which the believer is enabled to "bear fruit for God" (verse 4). Further, in the second marriage relationship the Christian still serves God under the terms of His law, but in a new spiritual attitude (verse 6). When Christ frees us from our relationship with the flesh and joins us to His Spirit, the law is no longer a negative instrument of *condemnation* but a positive reminder of our *commendation.*

The Paradox of Impotent Power

We see the paradoxical function of the law further illustrated in other sections of Paul's writings. Immediately after the marriage analogy, he utilizes a deductive argument to make it clear that the law has abiding significance (verses 7-12). I find it strange that those who see the marriage analogy as a repudiation of the law so frequently skip over the passage. Paul is obviously aware that some may misunderstand what he says about the law in the marriage analogy, so he starts this section with the rhetorical question "What then should we say? That the law is sin?" (verse 7). After denying such a possibility in the most emphatic way, he begins to explain how God's law functions.

Paul is clear that the main role of the law is to define sin (verse 7). The example he utilizes leaves no room for confusion. If the ten-commandment prohibition against covetousness did not exist, people who coveted would have no objective way of telling that their actions went against the will of God (verse 7). Notice that he did not say that there is no such thing as "covetousness"—he simply asserts that in the absence of the Ten Commandments we would have no standard to define such behavior as sinful. In one sense, then, the law *empowers* us to identify sinful actions. Unfortunately, the law's ability to do that also means that it serves as a powerful instrument of spiritual condemnation, since "the wages of sin is death" (Rom. 6:23).

Romans 5 graphically illustrates the role of the law in evoking condemnation. Here Paul describes the law as a powerless victim of sin's conniving strategy. From the perspective of the history of salvation, "sin was indeed in the world before the law" (verse 13). The fact that millions of people died before the giving of the law indicates the presence of sin, since death is the direct result of sin (verse 14). The revelation of God's moral code on Sinai did not introduce the concept of sin, but exposed it. Paul declares that when "law came in, . . . the trespass multiplied" (verse 20). Hence, as Paul pens our collective autobiography he laments, "Sin, seizing an opportunity in the commandment, produced in [us] all kinds of covetousness" (Rom. 7:8).

A more potent analogy appears in another passage in which Paul states, "The sting of death is sin, and the power of sin is the law" (1 Cor. 15:56). Here he depicts death as a poisonous creature whose venom consists of a sin-derived concoction. However, although death may take the form of a terrifying cobra, when you examine it closely it is as fangless as a charmer's snake. It possesses the potential to cause deadly harm, but lacks the means to infuse the venom into its opponent. Hence the usurped role of law, which provides the teeth that act as the intravenous needles through which the venom flows, resulting in the permanent paralysis of the sinner.

Given the role of the law in God's penal process, I can understand why so many Christians are upset with it. However, they have seriously misplaced their anger. Remember, the cobra's hollow fangs are merely instruments through which the venom flows. They serve the same purpose as the hypodermic needles that deliver the antivenom. To use another example, if I received a traffic ticket while speeding through a 15-mile-per-hour school zone, does it make any logical sense to get angry with the police officer? As Paul illustrates on a number of occasions, the problem does not lie with the law, but with sin. Rather than getting upset with the reflection in the mirror, I need to focus on the subject of the reflection. It's easy to blame the law, because it's so difficult to acknowledge that the real problem—sin—resides in us. The law merely reminds us of our own deplorable condition.

Reversing the Curse

It is in the light of the law's condemning function that we must understand Paul's referring to it as "the law of sin and death" (Rom. 8:2). The law is not inherently sinful and deadly. In fact, Paul has already declared that "the law is holy, and the commandment is holy and just and good" (Rom. 7:12). Sin may have hijacked the law for its own purpose, but we must never forget that every letter and diacritical mark contained in the law has a divine source. Anyone who relegates law to the dump heap has either consciously or unconsciously chosen to side with Satan. Satan may have "seized an opportunity" in the law and pulled us into sin even before we knew what sin was, but the law is and will always be a reflection of God's righteousness.

As Christians who truly desire a full relationship with our Maker we must be honest enough to admit that our spiritual nature has a lot to do with how we relate to the law. In fact, it is the brokenness in our spiritual nature that transforms the "holy, righteous and good" (NIV) law into one of "sin and death." As Paul carefully details in Romans 7:13-24, the negative function of the law has a direct link to our tendency to rebel against God. The truth is, before we even knew how to articulate our thoughts, Satan had already embedded the rebellious principles of his law into us. For every "thou shalt not," he has a "thou shalt." Consequently, the struggle between good and evil that commenced in the very courts of heaven finds a new battleground in each individual who has ever lived. As I stated before, our enemy is not the engraved stone tablet that convicts us of our pitiable state, but the satanic outpost that he has cunningly structured in our very nature.

As he reflected on the spiritual dilemma in which those who wish to serve God find themselves, Paul makes a desperate plea: "Wretched man that I am! Who will rescue me from this body of death?" (verse 24). Paul is well aware that the root of his wretchedness is the sinful nature that makes him an enemy to the law. He also understands that sinful tendencies cannot be controlled simply by a spiritual switch that we can turn on or off. Like David, he acknowledged, "Indeed, I was born guilty, a sinner when my mother conceived me" (Ps. 51:5). An honest analysis of his life led him to understand the words of Isaiah: "We have all become like one who is unclean, and all our righteous deeds are like a filthy cloth" (Isa. 64:6). After confronting the resurrected Christ and seeing beyond his pharisaical piety, Paul himself would admit, "all have sinned and fall short of the glory of God" (Rom. 3:23).

Furthermore, we must not forget that the wretchedness Paul laments is not based just on the fact that we are sinners, but on the reality that sin leads to death. As Romans 6:23 reminds us, the death to which Paul refers is not the fate that all post-Fall humans must face, but rather the death that robs us of the chance to spend a joyous eternity in the perfect presence of our Creator. For those who wish to experience full communion with God, the picture is even bleaker when we realize that there is no human fix for our spiritual dilemma. We can do nothing in our own power that will get us "in sync" with the law. I repeatedly run into people from the Abrahamic faiths who believe that they can do enough good deeds to gain God's favor. However, Paul makes it clear that "all who rely on the works of the law are under a curse; for it is written, 'Cursed is everyone who does not observe and obey *all the things* written in the book of the law'" (Gal. 3:10). The fact that everyone has missed that mark would mean that none qualifies for the kingdom.

Deliverance from the curse comes from a power beyond the law. The truth is, in the same way that the law may condemn but has no power to issue the death sentence, it is also impotent when it comes to acquitting the guilty. The only way a person can get on the same side as the law is by receiving a transformed nature that reflects the law's holiness. While such transformation is humanly impossible, the divine provision has been enabled through Christ who "redeemed us from the curse of the law by becoming a curse for us" (verse 13). The one who delivers us from the cursed "body of death" is "Jesus Christ our Lord!" (Rom. 7:24, 25). In removing the curse, Christ empowers us to embrace a new identity—one that reflects the very nature of the law. Hence Paul's exuberant declaration: "There is therefore now no condemnation for those who are in Christ Jesus. For the law of the Spirit of life in Christ Jesus has set you free from the law of sin and death" (Rom 8:1, 2). He continues, "For God has done what the law, weakened by the flesh, could not do: by sending his own Son in the likeness of sinful flesh, and to deal with sin, he condemned sin in the flesh, so that the just requirement of the law might be fulfilled in us, who walk not according to the flesh but according to the Spirit" (verses 3, 4). *This* is the gospel!

Conclusion

So what does Christ's death mean? As we have seen, some Christians believe that it signals the death of the law revealed on Sinai. Beguiled by Satan's lies, they have adopted the notion that the law is the basis of our sinful condition. They see the commandments as restrictive shackles given to make our life miserable. Christians who still hold on to the abiding moral significance of God's law get dismissed as legalists. Some even accuse them of spurning the grace of Christ. Little do they realize that they are singing verses from the same deceptive hymn that the cunning serpent rendered to Eve. Their message is the same: "Why should God tell you how to live? You are your own person and should be free to make your own decisions!"

Those who have relegated law to the archives of the archaic often call Paul to the witness stand. However, the "Paul" they have invented is not the apostle of Scripture. His appearance in the court of biblical interpretation would be detrimental to their argument. Rather than viewing the law as an irrelevant problem, he portrays it as an ally of Divinity Himself. As we see in Romans 7:13-24, it's not that we don't want to serve God on His terms, but that we have inherited rebellious tendencies.

The law does not cause our dilemma, but rather sin and its shameless willingness to contort the law for its own purposes. Although the law is the standard by which our sinful actions get judged, it has no power either to carry out the penalty for its violation or to acquit those who have received clemency. It is for this very reason that Jesus assumed our sin in His perfect body, died the eternal death for us, and was raised to an eternal life in which all faithful believers can participate. He has transferred us to the same righteous sphere in which law abides and has changed our status from the *condemned* to the *commended*.

My first permanent full-time job started out as a temporary assignment. With unemployment in England at the time hovering around 10 percent, I was elated when my supervisor informed me that management had offered to change my status. I worked in the quality-control division of the factory, and it was my responsibility to conduct performance tests on motors and tachometers. Having learned a lesson from my earlier work experience, I remained faithful to duty even in the absence of the supervisor and soon found myself entrusted with technical responsibilities for which I held no academic credentials.

Although I enjoyed what I did, I did not feel as though I was in the path that God had established for me. One day I surprised myself when I gave in to an overwhelming feeling to tender my resignation. I had no idea that the decision would take me in a completely different direction than what I had desired, but I knew I had to move on. Knowing that my supervisor would try to talk me out of it, I went straight to the manager, and after hearing my explanation he offered me his blessings. As per company policy, the resignation would not become effective for two weeks. I must admit that it was a temptation just to take it easy until I left. However, I knew I was being paid for a job, and although I was about to leave, I had an obligation to the company. For those final two weeks I made it a point to get to work on time and complete every task assigned to me with the competence to which my employers had become accustomed.

We must never forget that Christ's death does not free us from our obligation to keep the law but instead gives us a reason to obey it. When we were imprisoned by sin, God's law was indeed a "law of sin and of death," but now that Christ's righteousness has released us, it is instead the "law of the Spirit of life" (Rom. 8:1). The death of Christ has liberated us to engage in full communion with God even with our warts and failures! He invites us to draw near to His perfect holiness even in our imperfection. Even though we still bear the marks of sin, we are entrusted to honor His holy law.

---

[1] For example, Douglas Carson, ed., *From Sabbath to the Lord's Day: A Biblical, Historical and Theological Investigation* (Eugene, Oreg.: Wipf and Stock, 1999).

[2] See discussion in Keith Augustus Burton, *Rhetoric, Law and the Mystery of Salvation in Romans 7:1-6* (Lewiston, N.Y.: Edwin Mellen Press, 2001), pp. 1-17.

[3] *Ibid.*, pp. 69-72.

[4] *Ibid.*, pp. 4-8.

[5] *Ibid.*, pp. 94-97.

[6] I have intentionally omitted the "aroused by the law." I will explain why in the next section.

CHAPTER 7

Christ the End of the Law

The qualifying examinations were by far the most challenging hurdles in my doctoral studies. At that time, Northwestern University's Doctor of Philosophy in Religious and Theological Studies degree was interdisciplinary. It meant that I could take no more than half of my courses at Garrett-Evangelical Theological Seminary, which served as the university's graduate school of theology. I already knew that I would concentrate in New Testament studies on the seminary side, and my research methodology led me to the Classics, Rhetoric, and History departments. After two years of rigorous coursework, I had to take six exams during four eight-hour days.

My primary area didn't raise too many challenges in the exams. I had worked as a research and teaching assistant for both examiners, and was pretty comfortable in the areas of New Testament backgrounds and New Testament hermeneutical method and exegesis. I was also excited about the classical rhetoric exam, which was my second major research area. But I was more concerned about the exams in classical Greek philology and Roman history. For the Greek section I would have to sight-translate and provide commentary for selected sections from Homer's *Iliad* and was surprised that it was not as challenging as I had anticipated (I don't know if I could do it now!). My biggest shock came in the history exam when I had to explain first-century Roman military strategy on the Danube River. I don't know what I wrote!

The qualifying exams do not end with the written portion. Two weeks after sitting them, candidates must then face their examiners for an oral inquisition. I still remember the Friday afternoon I descended into the basement of the United Library and made my way to the Keene Bible Room. My chair, Robert Jewett, sat at the head of the table, and Michael

Leff, James Packer, William Stegner, and John Wright sat two to a side. The empty chair opposite Jewett was obviously mine, and I did my best to exude a cool aura as I attempted to settle into the "hot seat." Everything was going smooth until Packer started questioning me about Roman military strategy on the Danube River. It was obvious that I had not answered the question to his satisfaction, and he was determined to squeeze the information out of me.

After a prolonged back-and-forth, I threw up my hands in surrender and told him that I had divulged everything I knew about the topic. Breaking the silence, Jewett requested that I leave the room while the committee deliberated my fate. About 15 minutes later the door to the Keene Bible Room swung open, and Robert Jewett emerged with a satisfied look on his face. My skill as a mind reader was confirmed when I resettled into the "hot seat" and heard his affirming words, "Congratulations, you are now a candidate for the Doctor of Philosophy degree."

Although the qualifying examinations presented the most challenging hurdles, they were by no means the final ones. After the committee had approved my proposal, I still had to write the dissertation and meet with the committee once more to defend it. Sensing my nervousness, Jewett reminded me that I knew more about my topic than anyone else in the room. Each committee member fielded his questions, and by God's grace I was able to provide coherent answers. In fact, it was Jewett who posed the most challenging question, and while I paused to frame an answer, another committee member liked the question so much that he began to answer it before I tagged him out! About halfway through the scheduled time, the committee members looked at each other, and the chair asked me to leave the room. Moments later he emerged with that telltale expression on his face. Once settled, I was once more affirmed with three beautiful words: "Congratulations, Dr. Burton!"

Unfortunately, some interpret such a response as the end of a journey. However, it is really the beginning. The professional credentials provide access into an academy of scholars in which one can use the years of academic training with a sense of authority. When a reputable and accredited school provides the stamp of approval on a candidate, it is saying the graduate has mastered a body of knowledge that has earned them the right to become peers with their former teachers. With the successful completion of their studies, the relationship changes. However, they must never forget that their future success in their area of discipline is guaranteed only if they remember the principles their professors passed on to them. For the remainder of this chapter, we will discuss how the abiding principles of the law will always be a part of a grace-driven relationship with Jesus Christ.

The Faith of Christ

Years ago my dear friend, Pastor Robert Yee, shared with me that we could regard the word "grace" as an acronym for "God's redemption at Christ's expense." Indeed, this profound truth is the very essence of the gospel. Through Adam's sin the entire human race entered a state of brokenness that instantly distanced us from the presence of our Creator. The being once known as the heavenly light-bearer had deceived God's appointed landlord into giving him the deed to his dominion. In a lustful moment, Adam had bequeathed his descendants a life of terror, misery, and death. It was a hostile takeover executed through shrewd deception, and it cursed the inhabitants of the earth with an internal turmoil evoked by dueling allegiances to forces of good and evil. As a result, what we can describe only as spiritual schizophrenia has seized the human race.

God had created our primal progenitors with conditional immortality, and it was never His intention for them to experience death. However, in order for them to fulfill God's plan, it was necessary for them to maintain their nascent naiveté. Rather than overburden them with a detailed legal volume, the Creator gave our foreparents a simple command to refrain from associating with a tree. I suspect the garden had scores of trees, many laden with flavorful fruits that our minds could not now even imagine. Additionally, the countless animal species could have probably occupied their attention for millennia. Nonetheless, it was that forbidden tree that the serpent used as a prop to challenge the fairness of God's law, and the rest is painful history.

The Eden experience is a potent example of the power of sin. Why in the world would two people who had everything give it all up for the one thing that was off-limits? It doesn't seem to make sense. Nonetheless, throughout history the same scenario has repeated itself multiple billions of times. Somehow Satan successfully entices us into believing that our ultimate fulfillment depends on experiencing that which God has forbidden. The devil's supernatural ability to penetrate our innermost spirit has us torn between two masters. Unfortunately, those two masters treat us in completely opposite ways. Satan holds us by force and teases us into submission with periodic spates of instant gratification, while Christ values our free will by gently wooing us with the promise of an eternal joy that will never be in need of a "fix."

In a very real way Satan's ability to hold so many captive in his lair results from the way in which he has distorted the purpose of God's law. He does not portray it as the transcript of the divine character, but castigates it as an obstacle to happiness. In his world of debased passion and impulsive decisions, anarchy rules, and all do what is right in their own eyes. The devil has even been successful in promoting hybrid forms of this heretical teaching that manifest themselves in religiously shrouded self-righteousness and hypocrisy. Some limit the tenets of God's law, such as when they view 1 John 3:4 strictly in terms of the Ten Commandments. When John defines sin as "the transgression of the law" (KJV), he has not only the Decalogue in mind, but every action that violates God's eternal law of love and liberty. After all, God's law is purposed to maintain loving harmony in all of our relationships.

It is because of our brokenness and demonstrated inability to reflect the divine ideal that the Son of God entered our world. Divinity knew that if we were left to our own devices, the future would get only bleaker. Indeed, we see the decadence in society increasing by the day. In many ways it appears as if we are reliving the antediluvian narrative in which the Holy Spirit has become weary of warning the masses who have flippantly dismissed His urgent pleas. Nonetheless, it was for this generation—and those before it—that the Son of man left His heavenly splendor to provide a ransom with His blood. He was the Christ who would expend Himself for the redemption of humanity and was the embodiment of grace.

The biblical witness makes it clear that Christ's coming was not just about a sacrifice. If it were simply a matter of appeasing the Father with the blood of the Son, there would have been no need for Joseph and Mary to avoid Herod's sword by taking the newborn Babe to Egypt. However, Christ came to reverse the curse introduced into our world as a result of Adam's sin (Rom. 5:15-17). As the Second Adam, He would succeed where the original Adam failed. Adam's failure resulted from his disobedience, while Christ's success would stem from His obedience. In an efficacious act of humility and submission, Divinity would be transformed into a slave and subject Himself to the very law that He gave to humans. Scripture declares that His faithful obedience culminated in death (Phil. 2:5-8). He was not just a sacrifice—He was the perfect sacrifice.

As we reflect on what Jesus did for humanity, we must never forget the role of the law in the plan of salvation. Think about it: Jesus' religious life fueled the saving power of His death. By His own testimony He had kept

His Father's commandments and had continuously abided in His love. We can best appreciate the significance of His perfection when comparing it to the effects of Adam's corruption. The collective broken human condition is the result of one person's sinful actions. Through no act of our own we were all born with a death sentence. Our sin is not the same in gravity as Adam's, but we have to pay for it nonetheless. Adversely, Jesus' perfect life has universal implications for earth's inhabitants. His complete faithfulness has made His righteousness and the resultant eternal life available for all. It would not be wrong to say that we had been disadvantaged by Adam's sin, but those who believe the gospel should rejoice at the fact that through His life and death, Jesus has provided us with an advantage (Heb. 4:14-16).

Paul probably has this in mind when he declares that believers have been saved by the "faith of Jesus Christ" (e.g., Rom. 3:22; Gal. 3:16, 18). Some Bible versions miss the point when they render the Greek as "faith in Jesus Christ." I'm not sure why they chose to translate the Greek this way, particularly since "faith of Jesus Christ" is the more obvious meaning.[1] Through the phrase Paul emphasizes the fact that it is Jesus' faithfulness that made our salvation possible. His unflinching commitment to His Father's law enabled Him to enter death's chambers with our sins on Him but no sin in Him. He redeemed us from the curse of the law, not by destroying the law, but by vindicating it in the sight of the one who had abused it for his purpose. Through His fidelity, Jesus demonstrated to the universe that God's "law is holy, and the commandment is holy, righteous and good" (Rom. 7:12, NIV).

Our Legal Obligation

The fact that Jesus perfectly kept the law *for* fallen humanity has some serious implications for our relationship with God's law. Unfortunately, many Christians view it in ways difficult to support from a balanced reading of Scripture. The common view held by a significant number of evangelical Christians is known as *dispensationalism*. It is the belief that God's requirements for His people vary with historical and cultural "dispensations."[2] Perhaps the most popular aspect of the theory is the teaching that before Jesus came to earth, the Jews were under a dispensation of the law, but the establishment of the Christian church introduced the dispensation of *grace*. As a result, Christians under the dispensation of *grace* do not have to observe Old Testament laws. We see the implications of this stance in the belief that "one who worships on Sunday instead of Saturday is . . . a dispensationalist, because he recognizes the Sabbath was for Israel, not the church."[3]

From a biblical perspective, while it is true that the crucifixion of Christ put an end to the Temple sacrifices, nowhere in Scripture does it say that the people of God no longer need to observe His divine law. Those who hold such a position have chosen to ignore the fact that Israel's problem was the same as that of the Christian church and of every other religious organization: sin has affected and infected all of humanity. As we discussed in the previous chapter, we cannot solve the problem by doing away with the law. Sin is sin even if there is no law (Rom. 7:7). The law merely allows us to identify sin. Even before God presented the law at Sinai, the divine principles were well established among human beings.[4] Contrary to dispensationalist thought, they remain in effect even after the death of Christ.

We must never forget that God never intended for grace to free us from our obligation to observe His moral law. Instead, it serves as a powerful motivator for Christians to stay on the path of righteousness even after they have made mistakes, a truth graphically displayed in our collective autobiographical statement that Paul penned in Romans 7:13-25. In the discussion in the previous chapter, we looked at the passage from the perspective of the law as an instrument of condemnation. However, the fact that it *functions* negatively in no way negates the positive way in which the apostle describes it. Paul commences his discussion by asking, "Did what is *good*, then, bring death to me?" (verse 13). Later on he admits, "I agree that the law is good" (verse 16). He even confesses that although he misses the mark, "I delight in the law of God in my inmost self" (verse 22). The way in which Paul speaks of the law in this passage would make no sense if he intends to celebrate its abolition.

I cannot overstate the fact that Paul does *not* identify the problem as the law, but *sin*. Listen again to what he says in his narrative: "Did what is good, then, bring death to me? By no means! It was sin, working death in me through what is good, in order that sin might be shown to be sin, and through the commandment might become sinful beyond measure" (verse 13). This teaching is so obvious in the New Testament, but Satan has conducted a highly successful propaganda campaign that has led millions to believe that the law is our enemy. Somehow, he has blinded them to the texts that speak to the holiness and righteousness of the law, and they have become fixated on those that highlight the role of the law in condemning sinners.

Central to our discussion is an explanation of what Paul means when he states that "sin will have no dominion over you, since you are not under law but under grace" (Rom. 6:14). A dispensationalist reading views this as a declaration that God has introduced a new path to salvation. However, when viewed in context, it becomes clear that Paul is not talking about different methods or eras of salvation but is merely stating a fact. When a person dies to sin through the body of Christ, they are no longer subject to the law's condemnation, because righteousness now reigns in their heart (verses 1-14).

Knowing that some will misunderstand his statement about law, Paul quickly asks a rhetorical question: "What then? Should we sin because we are not under law but under grace?" (verse 15). In other words, do we no longer have to keep the law? That would be the case if grace *replaced* the law, but grace was not provided for the purpose of nullifying the transcript of a godly character. The miracle of grace manifests itself in its ability to neutralize sin. Hence, in answer to his question he responds with his characteristic emphatic negation: "By no means! Do you not know that if you present yourselves to anyone as obedient slaves, you are slaves of the one whom you obey, either of sin, which leads to death, or of obedience, which leads to righteousness?" (verse 16). Rather than offering an excuse to ignore the law, grace provides an incentive for all to continue observing God's law. It has broken the barrier of condemnation and opened the floodgates of righteousness so that all may access eternal life in Christ Jesus our Lord (verse 23).

Pathway to Christ

Unfortunately, some Christians see the significance of keeping God's law but are confused about its purpose. Consequently, they have fallen into the trap of the Pharisees and view their adherence to the law's precepts as a pathway to righteousness. Some have even condensed the Ten Command- ments into one and believe that strict Sabbath observance "covers a mul- titude of sins" and is the only key that can open the gate to the kingdom! Such a legalistic perspective is just as unbiblical as the one that downplays the importance of the law in the life of those who have an authentic rela- tionship with God.

Paul addresses the legalism issue by comparing the spiritual experience of Gentile believers and Israelite legalists (Rom. 9:1-10:4). Before I continue, it is important to state that the apostle speaks in general terms for illustrative purposes only. While some may sense an anti-Semitic bias in his argument, we must not forget that he himself was a proud bearer of Israelite genes, along with the majority of Christians during the era when he wrote his letter to Rome.[5] With that in mind, we can return to the comparison in which he states, "Gentiles, who did not strive for righteousness, have attained it, that is, righteousness through faith; but Israel, who did strive for the righteousness that is based on the law, did not succeed in fulfilling the law" (Rom. 9:30, 31). Again, it is important to remember that Paul is not saying that *every* Gentile has it right, and every Israelite had it wrong. He is simply comparing different approaches to salvation, and—as we see in Galatians—even some Gentiles resorted to works of the law as a pathway to righteousness.

While a surface reading of the passage may make it seem as if Paul is repudiating the law, that is far from reality. On the contrary, he does not stop his discussion with an indictment against Israel, but provides the reason for the futility in their approach. Utilizing his characteristic rhetorical style, he asks the question "Why not?" before explaining that Israel did not succeed in fulfilling the law, "because they did not strive for it on the basis of faith, but as if it were based on works" (verse 32). Notice that he had absolutely no problem with Israel's desire to keep the law. Instead, his disappointment stemmed from the fact that they saw the law as an instrument that could *make* them righteous. Not wishing to totally discredit their efforts, he writes, "I can testify that they have a zeal for God, but it is not enlightened. For, being ignorant of the righteousness that comes from God, and seeking to establish their own, they have not submitted to God's righteousness" (Rom. 10:2, 3). In other words, they may have had good intentions, but the only righteousness that leads to salvation is the one that originates from the Savior. Although the law contains the will of God, He never intended it to bestow righteousness.

When viewed through the perspective of grace, the law is an instrument that *points* us to righteousness. Hence Paul's statement: "Christ is the end of the law so that there may be righteousness for everyone who believes" (verse 4). At first glance, his statement seems puzzling, particularly the part that declares Christ as the "end" of the law. The English term *end* has the sense of "cessation" or "termination."[6] However, the Greek word used here is *telos*, better understood as "goal," "fulfillment," or "completion." He is the one to whom the law points and who fulfilled its requirements. The law is righteous but is not *righteousness*. As the embodiment of righteousness, Christ alone is its source for all who seek it.

When he discusses the topic in Galatians, Paul drives home the reality that God never meant the law to be an avenue for righteousness. He writes: "If a law had been given that could make alive, then righteousness would indeed come through the law" (Gal. 3:21). He then goes on to explain how the law functions by comparing it to a *paidagōgos* (verses 24, 25). Bible translators, struggling to find a suitable contemporary term for the Greek word, have chosen such options as "disciplinarian" or "schoolmaster." However, a *paidagōgos* in antiquity was an educated slave entrusted with the responsibility of training and instructing a nobleman's son. It was his responsibility to prepare the boy for manhood and life. While under his tutelage, the *paidagōgos* had the authority to do whatever it took to ensure that the son learned his lessons, and even had the authority to apply physical discipline. However, once the son reached maturity, the work of the *paidagōgos* was complete.

Maturity for the believer is symbolized by the justification (righteousness) that comes from Christ (verse 24). As *paidagōgos*, the law teaches us how to *live* right, but only Jesus can empower us to *be* right. The law demonstrates how a child of God ought to behave, but Jesus makes us children of God through His faithfulness (Gal. 3:26; 4:4, 5). Although the law points to Christ, there is never a time when it loses its importance. Utilizing the example of the *paidagōgos*, it would be a mistake to assume that his role was temporary. He may not have had the same level of control over the son, but ancient society expected that his former ward would have so absorbed his teachings that right living would be second nature. Similarly, those who have found righteousness in Christ are forever conscious of the righteous law that guided them to the Source of righteousness.

Conclusion

Those who ignore the important role of the law in the plan of salvation will never fully appreciate what Christ has done for us. The self-existent One through whom everything was created chose to enter our sinful reality to fulfill a mission of grace. Ultimate justice demands that sinful humanity receive the payment for its sins. God has the full prerogative to declare, as He did in the age of Noah, "I will erase humanity from the face of the earth" (see Gen. 6:7). But His very essence exudes a love that refuses to let us go. That love compelled the Son to identify with humanity and to walk a path that none has been able to travel. His omnipotence limited by sinful flesh, the incarnated Christ yielded fully to His Father and was perfectly obedient to His law.

Christ's obedience did not result from a selfish desire to show us that if *He* could do it *we* can too. He knew that our best efforts would always fall short. Nor did He come to compete *with* us. Rather, He sought to compete *for* us (Rom. 8:3). We were victims of Adam's failed encounter with the seductive serpent and had inherited a disadvantage in our sinful natures. In a sense, we were unwitting participants in a high-stakes "winner takes all" challenge. When we understand Adam's role in creating our dilemma, we can better grasp why Jesus came. In His incarnation He did not intend to show us how to save ourselves—we could never do that! Instead, He leveled the playing field. He came to ensure that every one of us would once again be spiritually prepared to participate in God's original plan for humanity. Consequently, when He succeeded where Adam failed by resisting the devil's temptation, the "winner takes all" rule meant that we were redeemed from the curse of sin (Rom. 5:12). Indeed, "in Christ God was reconciling the world to himself" (2 Cor. 5:19).

Since we have been reconciled to God, we have an opportunity to experience a genuine relationship with Him. It is not one based on fear, but one driven by love (1 John 4:18). Because we love Him, we have no problem abiding in His will. Hence, the law that was our enemy has become our friend. Instead of sin, righteousness now controls our inner core. Like the psalmist, we learn to delight in the law of the Lord (Ps. 1:2). True believers realize that the law is not the source of salvation, but the pathway to Christ—the *destination* of the law and the one who *is* our righteousness.

---

[1] For further study, see Richard Hays, *The Faith of Jesus Christ: The Narrative Substructure of Galatians 3:1-4:11*, 2nd ed. (Grand Rapids: Eerdmans, 2002).

[2] For an introduction to the dispensationalist theory, see P. P. Enns, *The Moody Handbook of Theology* (Chicago: Moody Press, 1989), pp. 513-526.

[3] *Ibid.*, p. 520.

[4] For instance, see discussion on Abimelech in K. A. Burton, *The Blessing of Africa: The Bible and African Christianity*, pp. 93-95.

[5] See James Dunn, *The Partings of the Ways: Between Christianity and Judaism and Their Significance for the Character of Christianity*, 2nd ed. (Norwich: SCM Press, 2011).

[6] For a detailed discussion, see Robert Badenas, *Christ the End of the Law: Romans 10:4 in Pauline Perspective* (Sheffield, London: Sheffield Academic Press, 1985).

CHAPTER 8

The Law of God and the Law of Christ

Less than a month after completing the requirements for my Doctor of Philosophy degree in November 1994, my family moved to Huntsville, Alabama, where Oakwood University had invited me to serve on the religion and theology faculty at Oakwood University. My wife and I were excited about returning to the place where we had first met in Professor E. O. Jones's Life Science class. As parents of two infants, we also felt privileged to be located in a city that experts claimed was the best in the United States to raise children. When we arrived, the weather was still relatively mild. It was a welcome relief from the freezing Chicago winters with the mounds of snow that had been our regular seasonal reality for seven years.

The balmy breezes of spring soon overwhelmed the short Alabama winter, and the carefully crafted landscape on the Oakwood campus confirmed our delight at returning to our alma mater. Life was good! In fact, we were enjoying it so much that we forgot that Huntsville's temperate climate resulted from its convenient location that was not too southerly and not too northerly. Consequently, when the moist southerly air seeks to introduce warm weather to the Northern states, the chilly dry northerly air begins to push back. At times the clash between the two weather extremes is so violent that it results in terrifying tornadoes. Huntsville just happens to be located in the region of the country whose name betrays the reason for its notoriety: Tornado Alley.

By May 1995 we began to question our relocation decision that had seemed a no-brainer less than seven months before. On the eighteenth day of that memorable month an F4 tornado touched down in the neighboring town of Harvest and caused major damage in the Anderson Hills community, where a number of Seventh-day Adventists resided. The cruel winds totally destroyed many homes and killed one person. I can still hear the late W. C. Jones testifying about how the tornado forced its way through his front door, sucked him up from his foyer floor, and dropped him naked and unconscious on the deck at the back of his severely damaged house!

It did not take long for things to get back to normal in Huntsville, and time quickly tamed the terror caused by the tornado. In fact, I didn't even think twice when my wife suggested that rather than buy a previously occupied house, we should probably build one in a new Harvest subdivision located about a mile from the recently afflicted Anderson Hills. That was four years after that dreadful day, and although many tornado warnings had sounded since then, no more had actually touched down. Sensing no real danger, I settled comfortably into my home and even learned to tune out the seasonal tornado sirens, which always seemed to go off at the very moment I had slipped into sweet slumber. If it were not for my fatherly and husbandly responsibility of providing a calming presence for my wife and children as we bedded down on the vinyl-covered concrete floor of the safe room, I would have stayed on my quilted mattress!

Twelve years after moving into our home, my relaxed attitude would change as I came face to face with reality. April 25-28, 2011, the United States experienced the largest tornado outbreak in recorded history. The third day was the deadliest, with an estimated 205 touchdowns resulting in more than 300 deaths and causing billions of dollars in damage. Once again tornadoes devastated Anderson Hills along with several other neighborhoods in the Huntsville Metropolitan area. In some communities not a single home remained standing. The storm came very close to our home, decimating the original structure of Ford's Chapel United Methodist Church (the oldest Methodist house of worship in the state of Alabama), which was less than a half mile away. We suffered minor damage, but nothing to the extent of so many people in our county.

After a couple days of helping in relief efforts and setting up a survival plan for the family, we decided to head to Georgia to stay with my sister-in-law until things got better. The electricity was down, and news sources estimated that it would be two weeks before the lines would be back up. Bracing for the worst in the aftermath, the mayor had urged all citizens who had friends or family in areas not hit to seek refuge there. Along with the fact that we had some genuine family health concerns, the mayor's urging helped to make our decision easier. Nonetheless, the farther I drove away from Huntsville, the more I felt as if I were deserting a sinking ship when hands were still needed on deck.

Guilt compounded my uneasy feeling when I showed up at my sister-in-law's church fully dressed in my Sabbath best. As I entered the foyer, I encountered some members in work clothes. They informed me that they were leaving to help a nearby community destroyed by the same tornado whose damage we had fled. I don't even remember who preached that day or anything else about the service. All I could think about was the devastated families and communities who had no place to call home. Did God really want me in the sanctuary when people nearby at that very moment were trying to figure out what to do for food and shelter?

I discussed my concerns with my family and received permission to return home with a friend. Eventually, after discovering that another family friend had electricity restored and could accommodate our health concerns, we all decided to return. Although it would be three days before our own home once again had power, we found several opportunities to help relieve the pain of those who suffered. When the next Sabbath came around, we worshipped together as a family at home, then put on jeans and comfortable tops and went into a hard-hit community. There we connected with a local relief organization and offered assistance to whoever needed it. Yes, this was the Sabbath of the Lord, but do we really believe that the Lord of the Sabbath hears the professed praise of hard-hearted worshippers who have deafened their ears to the cries of the hungry, homeless, and hurt? Did He really expect us to "get our praise on" that week when so many of our neighbors were mourning their losses? In this chapter we will discuss how the law of Christ helps us to better understand the law of God—indeed, they are one and the same.

Love and Legalism

Reacting to the formality of the mainstream Christian denominations from which they hailed, early Seventh-day Adventists adopted an anti-creedal position. Church pioneer John N. Loughborough explained the opposition to creeds in an early edition of the *Review and Herald*: "The first step of apostasy is to get up a creed, telling us what we shall believe. The second is to make that creed a test of fellowship. The third is to try members by that creed. The fourth [is] to denounce as heretics those who do not believe that creed. And fifth, to commence persecution against such."[1] Inherent in their resistance was the belief that creedal statements eventually assume the authority of divine law and tend to distract believers from the real object of our faith.

Ardent students of the Bible and history, the pioneers had seen the way in which the compounding of laws had created religious systems that bore the Christian banner but in many ways were anti-Christ. I'm sure they were aware that statements of faith had a purpose. James White and Uriah Smith issued the first extensive list in 1872, but they prefaced even those propositions with the warning "This is not to secure uniformity." They did not want the fledgling church to fall into the same trap as had so many of their predecessors whose efforts to reform Christianity had only created new legalistic systems in which creeds challenged Christ and rules rivaled righteousness. If it were not for the need to explain certain beliefs held in common "by the majority," they would have been content to continue affirming their faith with the words "We, the undersigned, hereby associate ourselves together as a church, taking the name of Seventh-day Adventists, covenanting to keep the commandments of God, and the faith of Jesus." Nonetheless, they put forth their propositions with the hope that they would not become legalistic barriers to salvation.

As far as the Adventist pioneers were concerned, the core instructions for Christian behavior were embodied in the commandments of God. Although they probably had the Decalogue in mind, I'm sure they would agree that the law of God is much more expansive. In fact, in the Sermon on the Mount Jesus declares that He has no intention of abolishing the law *and* the prophets. He knew that Scripture had divine commands that may not be explicitly stated in the tables that God revealed to Israel through Moses. For instance, the seventh commandment prohibits the sexual sin of adultery, but none among the 10 addresses bestiality, pederasty, pornography, homosexuality, or pre-marital sex. Additionally, it is the latter prophets who expound on God's disdain for cutthroat capitalism, wealth inequality, corrupt politics, and other issues of societal injustice.

Nonetheless, in spite of the scores of biblical laws that comprise the *total* law of God, it is the 10 upon which He based His covenant with Israel. Perhaps He intended them to be a set of principles that would serve as the basis for all other biblical laws. For example, the commandment prohibiting adultery assumes the marriage of a man and a woman, which indirectly speaks to premarital sex and homosexuality. Further, the tenth commandment's prohibition against covetousness can easily serve as a category that incorporates issues of predatory capitalism, corruption, and injustice. Indeed, it is probably in light of its ability to provide a general overview for most biblical laws that when Jesus cites the necessary commandments for those on the path to eternal life, he quotes from the Decalogue (e.g., Matt. 19:16-22).

Although Jesus obviously held the Ten Commandments in high esteem, it would be a mistake to view them as the simplest expression of divine law. In another place, He reveals that one could further reduce the law to two principles, which in essence are really *one!* When responding to a lawyer's inquiry about the greatest commandment, He replied: "You shall love the Lord your God with all your heart, and with all your soul, and with all your mind. . . . And a second is like it: You shall love your neighbor as yourself" (Matt. 22:37-39). It is difficult to miss the common denominator in both commandments: *love.* Jesus doesn't conclude His answer with the identification of the greatest commandments, but further qualifies: "On these two commandments hang *all* the law and the prophets" (verse 40). In other words, if you take either of them away, you have absolutely nothing!

Those who have committed to keeping God's commandments have continuously to remind themselves about the centrality of love. Sometimes we can get so distracted by the "what" of commandment keeping that we forget about the "why." Perhaps that is the reason that in His final discourse with His disciples Jesus told them, "I give you a new commandment, that you love one another. Just as I have loved you, you also should love another. By *this* everyone will know that you are my disciples, if you have love one for another" (John 13:34, 35). As José Vicente Rojas likes to preach, we can fully appreciate the commandments only when we see them through the lenses of loving relationships. One who loves God wouldn't want to break His heart by lusting after idols, taking advantage of Him, or ignoring His weekly appointments with us. Similarly, those who love their fellow human beings will be respectful to parents, express loving fidelity to spouses, honor the right for others to live, and be content with what they have. When we understand that God's law is there for our benefit, we will never condemn this symbol of love as a vehicle of legalism.

Accommodation and Compromise

I suspect that many people experience difficulty keeping God's law because they view it as a punitive prison guard rather than a public safety officer, whose responsibility is to protect and serve. The Lord revealed His law not to provide an obstacle to our spiritual progress, but to help us find the right path when we have strayed. God is so committed to our spiritual success that He does everything in His power to assist us in staying faithful to Him. In fact, it is the very reason that He gave us the law—He didn't want us to guess about His requirements. John reminds us: "For the love of God is this, that we obey his commandments. And his commandments are not burdensome" (1 John 5:3).

Anchored as they are in the patient principle of love, we find much latitude *in* God's commandments. Notice I did not say there is much latitude *with* them. The principles may be *expandable*, but they are definitely not *expendable*. Paul recognizes this when he shared his evangelistic strategy:

"For though I am free with respect to all, I have made myself a slave to all, so that I might win more of them. To the Jews I became as a Jew, in order to win Jews. To those under the law I became as one under the law (though I myself am not under the law) so that I might win those under the law. To those outside the law I became as one outside the law . . . so that I might win those outside the law. To the weak I became weak, so that I might win the weak. I have become all things to all people, that I might by all means save some. I do it for the sake of the gospel, so that I may share in its blessings" (1 Cor. 9:19-23).

The phrase that sticks out to some is the part that says: "to those under the law I became as one under the law (though I myself am not under the law)." On the surface, it sounds as if Paul is saying that the law is not really important.

Taken to the extreme, one could, for example, extrapolate that evangelism should reject no method. Armed with their questionable interpretation of the passage, some ministers have chosen strip bars and nightclubs as their place of ministry and have even adapted the behavior of those who patronize these establishments. If that were the entirety of New Testament teaching, I would have no quarrel with such an understanding. However, we must take two things into account. First, Paul uses the words "under the law" in this context to refer to his fellow Jews who sincerely believe that they derived salvation from their fidelity to the sanctuary service and strict observance of ceremonial laws (as opposed to non-Jews who are "outside the law"). Paul knows such beliefs are not essential to salvation, but as we see in Acts, he had no problem performing ceremonial rituals with his compatriots.

Second, and most important, it would be extremely difficult to extract such an interpretation from this passage. Those familiar with the text would have noticed that I deliberately omitted an essential parenthetical statement. In his explanation, just after Paul says that he becomes as one outside the law for those outside the law, he offers an important qualification: "though I am not free from God's law but am under Christ's law" (verse 21). In other words, Christ's law permits him to accommodate, but never to compromise the principles of God's law. Strangely, although Paul attributes distinct laws to the Father and the Son, the fact that they are complementary suggests their unity. It would not be a stretch to say that they are one and the same!

A person who has grasped the essence of what it means to keep God's law will never allow the law to become a barrier between the searching sinner and eternal life. Jesus Himself willingly became the subject of gossip in His desire to reach fallen humanity. According to the Gospels, after He had successfully recruited Matthew into His inner circle, He went to the new disciple's house for a meal with his friends (Matt. 9:10-13). Given the fact that Matthew was Jewish, that should not have been a problem. However, the man was a tax collector, and his friends were not very religious. As far as the Pharisees were concerned, a righteous person would never associate with such types. I'm sure their gossip contained the proverbs "Show me your company and I will show you who you are" and "Birds of a feather flock together." Notwithstanding, Jesus knew that He had not transgressed any of His Father's laws, and sent a message to them: "Those who are well have no need of a physician, but those who are sick. Go and learn what this means, 'I desire mercy, not sacrifice.' For I have come to call not the righteous but sinners" (verses 12, 13).

When people commit to the law of Christ, they will not allow others who have never done anything for the sake of the gospel to dictate their strategies for reaching people. Recently a missionary friend, who also happens to be a practicing vegan, addressed a small group of students going to a foreign mission field. Among the stories he told was an account of getting a stomach bug after eating undercooked chicken in a village. Yes, you did read it right! My friend *is* a vegan. Nevertheless, when he visited that impoverished village, he knew that the meal presented to him had been prepared at great expense and sacrifice. To reject the food would have been a great insult. Had it been on the forbidden list of unclean foods, he would have had no choice but to refuse it. However, there was no biblical reason to object, and so he partook of a small portion. Given his willingness to practice the law of Christ, it is probably no coincidence that a thriving church and school now exist in an area where no one had even heard the gospel message before his arrival.

Mercy and Justice

Some have no problem exercising flexibility with those being recruited into the church, but have zero tolerance with members who make mistakes. However, we must never forget that those members are subject to the same law of Christ that graciously accommodates nonbaptized sinners who wish to enter into relationship with God. Before I continue, please allow me to reiterate my continued refrain that the keeping of God's law is not optional for believers. Our freedom from the curse of the law does not give us an excuse to ignore it. In fact, the Bible attributes an enabling power to grace, which suggests that it is the force that makes our fidelity to the law possible. In his letter to Titus, Paul writes, "For the grace of God has appeared, bringing salvation to all, training us to renounce impiety and worldly passions, and in the present age to live lives that are self-controlled, upright, and godly" (Titus 2:11). Notwithstanding, even with grace on our side, at times we may still miss the mark.

Having struggled with sin from my earliest memories, I remember silently hoping as a young lad that when Jesus returns, it would not be at a moment I was doing something bad! Somehow I had the idea that a person could be alternately saved and lost several times in the same day. Everything depended on what they were "doing" at the time Jesus came to their name on the judgment list. I still hear people echoing this sentiment when someone dies. With philosophical certainty they declare that God knew that if such individuals continued living, they would have backslid, so He took them to guarantee their salvation. It would lead me too much off topic to address this, but such thought is born from the belly of a belief called "predestination."

Countering this line of thinking, Ellen G. White reminds us: "The character is revealed, not by occasional good deeds and occasional misdeeds, but by the tendency of the habitual words and acts."[2] In other words, people who are in the process of forming righteous habits may sometimes find themselves victims to sin, but it does not mean that they are automatically disqualified from the kingdom (1 John 5:16, 17). When addressing this topic, the legendary evangelist E. E. Cleveland would bellow in his raspy tone, "We are justified before we are qualified, we are accepted before we are acceptable, we are trusted before we are trustworthy, and we are declared perfect while we are being perfected."[3] As we learn to surrender our wills to the One who redeemed us, there *will* be times we transgress His law, but that does not alter the reality of our salvation.

Ironically, when believers fail in their relationship with God, it is the very law that they violated that reminds them of their need for restoration. It is out of his understanding of God's stubborn grace that Paul admonishes: "My friends, if anyone is detected in a transgression, you who have received the Spirit should restore such a one in a spirit of gentleness. Take care that you yourselves are not tempted" (Gal. 6:1). Here he appeals to our own susceptibility. While we have a responsibility to uphold righteous standards in the church, none of us is immune from temptation. Since we are all fighters on the field of life, we must never forget that our first response to an erring member is restoration, not repudiation. In fact, it is not even optional—it's a nonnegotiable mandate: "Bear one another's burdens, and in this way you will fulfill the law of Christ" (verse 2). Governed by the ultimate principle of divine law, we must obey God's call for all of us to support each other's desire to live in harmonious relationship with our Maker.[4]

As we discussed in previous chapters, the same law that encourages us to find our righteousness in Jesus Christ is the one that God will use as the standard of judgment. He has done everything in His power to ensure that every human who has ever lived has had an opportunity to accept His free gift of salvation. Even those who have never heard the gospel have had the same opportunity as those who were born, bred, and buried in the church (Rom. 2:14-16).[5] Given the extent to which the Lord has gone to guarantee our salvation, all who reject His grace have no one to blame but themselves, when He declares the end of probation with "Let the evildoer still do evil, and the filthy still be filthy, and the righteous still do right, and the holy still be holy" (Rev. 22:11).

Even as I write this chapter, I am positively overwhelmed by the extent of God's love toward us. Knowing that transgressors of the law could never inherit eternal life, He not only removed our transgressions, but also provided the means for us to remain in harmony with the law through the faithfulness of His Son. His gracious actions vindicate the very purpose of His law, which reflects the principles of loving relationships. Having demonstrated His love in a tangible way, His final judgment on us is based on our willingness to be possessed by that same love. John declared, "God is love, and those who abide in love abide in God, and God abides in them. Love has been perfected among us in this: that we may have boldness on the day of judgment, because as he is, so are we in this world" (1 John 4:16, 17).

Conclusion

In his commentary on the "royal law of liberty" (the Ten Commandments), James reminds us that "judgment will be without mercy to anyone who has shown no mercy; mercy triumphs over judgment" (James 2:13).

If only those trapped in legalism's lair could understand this. Rather than engaging in Bible study with the purpose of finding new laws to aid in the self-righteous quest for perfection, people who truly desire to do God's will should be combing the pages of His book with the earnest plea "Show me how to love as You do." Detecting the principle of love in each commandment should be the quest of every Christian. When our sin-warped minds have learned to realign God's law with His love, we will then know how to be channels of His love in our efforts to "rescue the perishing" and "care for the dying."

Several years ago I presented a paper at the Adventist Society of Religious Studies titled "The Missing Fundamental Belief: Love as the Key to Church Renewal." The paper pointed out that as a church we often like to talk about our distinctive doctrines, each of which serendipitously starts with the symbol "S": the Sabbath, the Second Coming, the Sanctuary, the State of the Dead, and the Spirit of Prophecy. While those teachings are important, without a commitment to the central biblical doctrine that starts with the letter "L," they mean absolutely nothing (1 Cor. 13).

Revelation defines God's end-time people as those who "keep the commandments of God and hold the testimony of Jesus" (Rev. 12:17). They are a people so committed to their relationship with the Lord that they will publically demonstrate their fidelity to Him, even if it means being castigated as a cult by those who have hijacked Christ's name to practice paganism. However, they also realize that the law of God to which they exhibit defiant obedience is inseparably fused to the law of Christ. Convicted of this reality, they understand that the true sign of the remnant's fidelity is the love that exudes from the heart of each individual (John 13:34, 35).

---

[1] John Loughborough, "Doings of the Battle Creek Conference, October 5 & 6, 1861," *Review and Herald* , Oct. 8, 1861.

[2] Ellen G. White, *Steps to Christ* (Mountain View, Calif.: Pacific Press Pub. Assn., 1956), pp. 57, 58.

[3] For Don Schneider's interview with E. E. Cleveland where he repeats his famous phrase, see video on http://youtu.be/t1AHrDlVHuQ.

[4] For a wonderful reminder of our supportive role in the church community, see Philip Yancey, *What's So Amazing About Grace?* (Grand Rapids: Zondervan, 2002).

[5] For a discussion on universal access to salvation, see the chapter "For God so Loved the World," in Keith Burton, *The Compassion of the Christ* (Grantham, Eng.: Stanborough Press, 2004).

CHAPTER 9

Christ, the Law, and the Gospel

My doctoral-degree years were extremely hectic and stressful. In addition to the coursework, I had a number of other priorities that demanded concentrated time. First was my brand-new bride, with whom I was being schooled in the unpredictable university of marriage. Another time divisor entered my equation with the birth of my firstborn, Sheereen. That little bundle of joy was a delightful distraction and the unpaid model for hundreds of photographs taken on my intemperate Olympus OM10 (many of the 35-millimeter rolls still undeveloped!). In addition to family responsibilities, I was serving as a volunteer pastor at the First Seventh-day Adventist Church of Evanston, whose delightful congregation is still a part of my life and family.

Of course, my family and I also had to eat and pay the bills, so I worked in a number of jobs. My primary one was as a research assistant to world-renowned scholar Robert Jewett, who also served as my *doktorvater* (a German term for a doctoral-degree supervisor) in more ways than one. Together we worked on collating a multilingual thematic bibliography that exceeded 1,000 pages on the biblical book of Romans! When the research dollars got thin, I secured nonacademic work through a temporary agency. My longest stint was working as a clerical assistant in a logistics company where I was responsible for researching, writing, and formatting weekly reports and then distributing them to top management. For the last period of my studies I served as the administrative secretary for the Center for the Church and the Black Experience at Garrett-Evangelical Theological Seminary, where I edited the CBE newsletter and had the privilege of an office next to the late United Methodist churchman and social activist Bishop Edsel A. Ammons.

In addition to family, pastoral duties, and regular work assignments, there were times I had the opportunity to make a little extra. Especially during the holiday season, my dear friend Anne-Marie would invite me to help out in her catering company. I would don my black suit, white shirt, and bow tie and drive to exquisite mansions in well-heeled towns such as Winnetka, Kenilworth, and Glencoe. There I spent my evenings serving food, picking up used glasses and plates, and helping the guests with their coats. At the end of the evening I could always anticipate a decent check—and it was not unusual to receive a three-figure tip! Needless to say, with so many nonacademic responsibilities I was often up late burning the midnight oil. A couple times I even had to "pull" the proverbial "all-nighter."

Perhaps the scariest moment during that period happened during the quarter when I took a class on the philosophy of Aristotle. My professor for the course was the late Reginald E. Allen, who was one of the world's most respected authorities on Aristotle. Prof. Allen had a rather unique style and rarely gave a lecture. He would come to class with a profound question and guide the discussion with more questions. If you were fortunate enough to engage him during the class's afterglow, you would catch a glimpse into his profound, yet humble, mind. He was a "walking encyclopedia," but was not "full of himself."

Although he was approachable, it was with fear and trepidation that I knocked on his office door that Monday. The main paper was due on Thursday, and I had not even started my research. The pressures of family, work, and school seemed to be pushing me underwater, and I needed time to breathe. I could not pass the class without the paper, but there was absolutely no way I could do a good job in the brief time that I had. Even today I still remember his response when I poured out my heart to him: "Mr. Burton, the paper is due on Thursday." I knew better than to challenge his principles, and left the office with my eyes looking heavenward. I had come too far to fail a class.

As I sat in the library wondering how to proceed, the Holy Spirit brought something to mind. My sole reason for taking the class was to try to understand Aristotle's mode of thinking as it related to his *philosophy* of rhetoric. In a previous quarter I had written a paper on the technical aspect of Aristotle's rhetoric for a class on Greek rhetorical theory. As I thought about the amount of time and effort I had put into that paper, I realized that I could easily apply some of the research to a philosophical context. All of a sudden, the task did not seem as daunting, and with the decreased pressure, I was able to competently complete a fresh paper for which I earned a satisfying A.

When Prof. Allen handed the paper to me, he had a look on his face that seemed to say, "I knew you could do it!" I had been making good grades in his class all along, and although he must have noticed my sense of despair, somehow he believed that I would have a paper on his desk on time. While I'm not sure if deep down he felt like giving me more time, he still had a standard to uphold and had to be fair to others in the class who may have had even more serious challenges than I. He could not compromise his rules to accommodate me—the paper had to be submitted. However, even before I sought for leniency, God had already provided an answer. All I needed to do was "be still" and allow Him to work. When I stopped worrying about everything I had to do and looked to Him for help, He allowed me to see that He had already worked out the answer to my dilemma. Empowered by His revelation of grace, I was able to satisfy the requirements of Prof. Allen's "law"! In this chapter we will discover how the biblical teaching on law and grace helps to provide a more complete picture of God.

The Law Revealed

When I approached Prof. Allen about giving me more time to complete an assignment, I knew that I was asking him to go against certain stipulations that he himself had put into place. When he wrote the course syllabus, he probably took several things into consideration. First, he must have thought about the fact that it was one of three courses that made up the full load for graduate students each quarter. Second, he would have ensured that the content of the course matched the intensity required for a terminal degree. Finally, he would have structured the course calendar in such a way that the assignment due dates were thoughtfully spaced to allow the students to do competent work.

As a university professor with academic freedom, he did not have to consult anyone about the content of his course or the way in which he arranged the class calendar. He was the expert, and the university expected that he possessed the knowledge and skills to prepare a syllabus. On the first day of class, when each student received a copy, there may have been a few raised eyebrows when we were contemplating the workload or grade distribution, but we knew that the document was nonnegotiable. We trusted that a man of Allen's repute was fully aware of what it took to raise us to a certain level of competence. By abiding by the terms of his syllabus, each person had an opportunity to complete the class successfully.

Although not often thought of as such, a syllabus is a legal document. Whatever the professors put on those pages becomes a contract between them and their students. The syllabus basically establishes what the teacher will do for the student, what the student must do in the course, and how the teacher will evaluate the student's performance. In a remarkably parallel sense it functions like the divine law that the Lord revealed to the world. God, the source of law, penned the contents and informed the recipients what to expect from Him. As the ultimate expert on human nature, He did not have to consult with anyone about the content for His law. His law is also very clear about what He requires from humans: love. Further, it stipulates the method by which one's performance gets evaluated.

Scripture does not record Him giving a law to any other people group during the years before the revelation of His written covenant at Sinai. Nonetheless, we do find strong evidence that the human family already had knowledge of His law. From a biblical perspective, it is clear that the patriarchs had a sense of right and wrong. For instance, Abraham was distraught when commanded to expel Hagar and Ishmael to what he at first thought was an uncertain future (Gen. 21:11-14). We also observe how Jacob struggled with guilt for betraying his brother (Gen. 32). Another instance is Reuben's compassion for Joseph, which stopped his brothers from killing him (Gen. 37:21, 22). The sense of morality was not limited to only the "chosen"—we see it displayed in people outside of God's special covenant. As we noted in a previous chapter, the Gerarite king, Abimelech, knew that he was not supposed to commit adultery (Gen. 20). Also, before his apostasy, Balaam appeared to have been a faithful prophet of God (Num. 22:12-21).[1] Further, the Egyptians and Babylonians had clearly defined moral laws in both the Book of the Dead[2] and the Code of Hammurabi.[3]

From the stories of Noah, Abimelech, Balaam, Abraham, Isaac, Jacob, and Joseph we learn that before God presented the revealed law it was not unusual for Him to make personal appearances to express His will. It is even possible that some of the moral laws among the Babylonians and Egyptians may have originated as supernaturally revealed commands that the people then contextualized and embellished. After all, every law that promotes loving relationships has its origin in God. However, with so many "versions" of purportedly divine law in circulation, it became necessary for Him not only to reveal an authorized version but to do it in such a magnificent way that none would deny that He was the sole source.

The method through which God revealed His law to humanity is a strong sign of its uniqueness. I suppose He could have picked representatives in the major geographical areas of the world and provided a copy of the law to each one. However, He chose to pick a man *and* a people to serve as types of the universal story of salvation. The enslaved Israelites may have been familiar with the oral law passed down from their ancestors, but they had no written way to determine God's will. The truth is, given their oppressed circumstance, even if they had a written document they probably would not have felt compelled to observe it.

In light of their situation, we can see why God called on Moses to lead the liberation struggle. Moses had grown up in the opulent chambers of Egyptian royalty before circumstances drove him into exile. It was while he was in exile that he received his marching orders from the voice emanating from the bush that burned but was not consumed. Returning to Egypt, he obeyed the voice of God and led his people to freedom. With the Red Sea separating them from the scourge of the slavemaster's whip, the newly liberated slaves began to savor the taste of freedom. Sensitive to their need for relief after years of working seven days a week from sunrise to sunset, their Creator also gave them a gentle reminder of His precious day on which nobody had to busy themselves with routine chores.

Life after emancipation was by no means smooth, as a people learned the difficult lesson of trusting in the very One whom they had silently questioned during their years in slavery. As they camped before Mount Sinai, God delivered a message of affirmation to them through His servant Moses: "You have seen what I did to the Egyptians, and how I bore you on eagles' wings and brought you to myself. Now therefore, if you obey my voice and keep my covenant, you shall be my treasured possession out of all the peoples. Indeed, the whole earth is mine, but you shall be for me a priestly kingdom and a holy nation" (Ex 19:4-6).

Think about it: God is speaking to a people who don't know Him well. They are still trying to shake Egyptian habits and struggling to overcome a slave mentality. It is upon these people that God places His priestly mantle and says, "I *trust* you to represent Me." They had experienced His love and power and now He was delegating to them the responsibility of channeling that same love and power. Having removed the oppressive shackles of slavery from their hands and feet, God now offers to liberate them from mental and spiritual bondage. It is in this emancipative setting that He offers the invitation that prefaces His revealed law: "I am the Lord your God, who brought you out of the land of Egypt, out of the house of slavery; you shall have no other gods before me" (Ex. 20:2).

The Law Perceived

Although God entrusted Israel with His law, He did not intend for it to be exclusively theirs. In fact, when He affirmed them, He let them know that they had a responsibility to the inhabitants of the world. Why else would He call them a "priestly kingdom" and a "holy nation" (Ex. 19:6)? Theirs was to be that shining city on a hill that would radiate the soft light of God's love so effectively that all the other nations would want what they had.[4] However, the God who created humans with the freedom of choice could not just will His plan into action. He needed the cooperation of those with whom He had covenanted. Each Israelite had a responsibility to be a channel of God's presence, and they could accomplish that only by staying in fellowship with Him—hence the irreplaceable role of the law.

Unfortunately, they were less than faithful in their part of the relationship. For reasons that are all too familiar to many of us, they could not grasp the seemingly simple notion that the law's purpose was to outline the terms of our relationship with God and not to show us how to gain His favor. They had already received their reward before He even asked them to observe His commandments. In fact, the Lord wanted them realize that faithfully obeying the commandments was the only way they could fully comprehend what He had done for them. Remember, the essence of the commandments is love, and as we read them through these lenses, it is not hard to see the divine plea for behavior that will produce healthy loving relationships between people and the rest of God's creation.

While the intention of the law was to create a loving environment in which people respected each other, God knew that a violation of His law would have the opposite effect on society. It is for this very reason that God defines consequences for lawbreakers. Establishing a law means nothing if it has no penalties for violating it. That has been clear from the very first command that God expressed to Adam in the Garden of Eden. Interestingly, when you analyze the biblical laws, it's not so much the stipulation that makes you shiver, but the penalty attached to it. Few would disagree that children should respect their parents or that spouses should be faithful to each other. It is clear to see how such admonitions contribute to a loving society. However, the thought of being stoned to death for those infractions is enough to make one forget why the law exists in the first place!

Although the descriptions of the penalties attached to the violation of the law are often gruesome, the penalties are necessary in a community setting. Known by the Latin term *lex talionis* (law of retaliation), such sentences seek to discourage those tempted to disrupt the order of the community. If there were no articulated and enforceable penalties, chaos would reign. In fact, it is for this very reason that all law-based societies attach negative consequences for illegal behavior. In light of this, it would be a gross distortion of the law's purpose to define it by its penalty. Godly derived laws intend not to inflict pain but to maintain harmony.

As we mentioned earlier, laws similar to those in the Bible "also appear in Mesopotamian legal collections, most notably in the Code of Hammurabi, and are fundamental to many ancient legal systems."[5] It is a clear indication that God has left no people group on the face of the earth without a witness. Some sections of those codes differed from the law given through Moses, but glimpses of truth were there for any honest seeker to grasp. We may never know the exact means by which such laws came to them, but we are told that even in a place as evil as Sodom "God in His mercy permitted rays of light to shine amid the moral darkness."[6]

Fortunately, God's plan of salvation did not depend on Israel's faithfulness. The fact that His chosen people failed to provide a practical example of His power did not thwart His overall plan. Licentiousness and legalism may have tainted their witness, but the loving principle behind God's law did not remain concealed from those outside the appointed circle. After His spiritually disturbing vision, the apostle Peter quickly came to terms with this reality and declared, "I truly understand that God shows no partiality, but in every nation anyone who fears him and does what is right is acceptable to him" (Acts 10:34, 35). Paul also discussed the ubiquitous presence of God's law: "When Gentiles, who do not possess the law, do instinctively what the law requires, these, though not having the law, are a law to themselves. They show that what the law requires is written on their hearts" (Rom. 2:14, 15). In spite of Israel's failure, many "heathens" will be among the faithful in the kingdom. Some may want to believe that knowledge of the revealed law is a prerequisite to salvation, but we must remember that "those whom Christ commends in the judgment may have known little of theology, but they have cherished His principles."[7]

The Law Applied

Since the Bible teaches that some will experience salvation without even knowing the content of the law, I could fully understand why a person would choose to question its importance. After all, if individuals can be saved after living all of their lives without keeping the Sabbath or refraining from idols, why should anyone observe the law? While such a line of reasoning is logical, from a biblical perspective it would be valid only if we did not possess a revelation of God's will. However, His holy law provides that revelation, and when the Spirit reveals it to someone, they will make adjustments if they are serious about their relationship with God. Paul solidifies this teaching in his famous sermon to the Stoic and Epicurean philosophers on the Areopagus when he announced, "While God has overlooked the times of human ignorance, now he commands all people everywhere to repent, because he has fixed a day on which he will have the world judged in righteousness by a man whom he has appointed" (Acts 17:30, 31).

The accommodation for Gentiles ignorant of the law reflects the same grace extended to those who know the law but find themselves "falling short" of God's glory. Such grace results from the faithfulness of Jesus, whose unwavering obedience to the requirements of His Father enabled our righteousness. It is only through Him that the righteous law can be applied to the hearts of those still engaged in a struggle against their (our) sinful nature. John sums up the act of divine mercy in one verse: "The law indeed was given through Moses; grace and truth came through Jesus Christ" (John 1:17).

The translators of the King James Version, Contemporary English Version, and Today's English Version totally distort the meaning of the text when they insert "but" before the word "grace." Their obvious intention is to draw a contrast between "law" and "grace." However, the original Greek has no adversative conjunction. In fact, there is no conjunction at all. Jesus' coming was not a backup plan implemented only if the first plan did not work. It was part and parcel of the *only* plan that ever existed. After all, isn't He the "Lamb that was slain from before the foundations of the world" (Rev. 13:8)? God knew exactly what He was doing when, through Moses, He entrusted Israel with the divine oracles (Rom. 3:2). The very law that those who misunderstand its purpose have slandered and maligned is on the same side as grace, and God gave it as a gift to prepare His people for eternity with Him.

God's ultimate promise is personified in Jesus, who is the mysterious manifestation of both law and grace. As law, He embodies righteousness and exudes the love that proceeds from His Father. And as grace, He embodies forgiveness fueled by the same love emanating from the One who sent Him for our redemption. An active participant in the plan of salvation, "God was in Christ, reconciling the world unto himself, not imputing their trespasses unto them" (2 Cor. 5:19, KJV). Jesus is the visible manifestation of God's justice and mercy, through whom we receive a glimpse of our Creator. John portrays it this way: "No person has ever seen God, but His only born Son who is intimately intertwined with Him has explained what His Father is all about" (see John 1:18).

Christ's explanation of His Father should be comforting news for the entire world. Through Christ Satan's lies about the nature of God and His law stand exposed. We are bombarded daily by the demonic propaganda machine that generates countless reminders about our failures. The father of lies receives further aid from self-righteous zealots trying to eat, study, and dress their way to the kingdom despite living under their own heavy cloud of guilt. Their onerous requirements have driven away many a person who refuses to associate with people so burdened by their beliefs. They view the law as a steep stepladder rather than a level learning path, and do their best to ensure that those mounting the ladder behind them will never overtake them. In their warped understanding of biblical faith, God is a punitive despot who demands unflinching compliance to His demands. However, the gospel provides a corrective. The law is not a dilapidated obstacle to reject, but a relevant partner to embrace. Further, God is not an exacting taskmaster testing our ability to pass an impassable test. Rather, "he is not willing that any of us should perish, but that all will come to repentance" (see 2 Peter 3:9). It is for this purpose that Jesus made it possible for us to become aligned with the law. It is pardon, not punishment, that God desires. Hence John declares, "God did not send His Son into the world to condemn it, but to save it" (see John 3:17).

Soon and very soon God will announce His judgment, and that day will produce a number of surprises. Many who have rejected God's transforming grace in favor of their own religious deviations will be denied access to the kingdom. At the same time, untold multitudes who had never even heard the word "Bible" will be counted among the faithful. I am fascinated by the way in which Ellen White paints the scene: "How surprised and gladdened will be the lowly among the nations, and among the heathen, to hear from the lips of the Savior, 'Inasmuch as ye have done it unto the least of these my brethren, ye have done it unto me!' How glad will be the heart of Infinite Love as His followers look up with surprise and joy at His words of approval!"[8]

Conclusion

Whether they know it or not, everyone will be judged by what the apostle James refers to as the law of liberty. The law that the Lord presented to the world through His servant Moses, it does not seek to make our lives difficult, but to provide a path to harmonious relationships with God, His creation, and our fellow human beings. The Lord desperately desires that those called by His name will be examples of the beloved community He envisions. Indeed, if the chosen faithfully kept His law, His church would be a delightful alternative to a world characterized by dark values. Unfortunately, those whom God has appointed have not always been faithful in witness. Both physical *and* spiritual Israel have let Him down.

Although God wants His church to portray a practical prototype of His kingdom, His comprehensive plan of salvation does not depend on this single element. The Holy Spirit does not limit His work to the confines of Christ's visible body, but continues to reveal God's will everywhere possible. The Spirit is continuously convicting people who have never heard of Jesus or Adam about God's loving principles, and they then serve as willing channels of His grace to their neighbors. Jesus knows the sincerity of their hearts, and although they are totally ignorant of the stipulations contained in the Ten Commandments, they *will* hear the blessed "well done" from His lips on judgment day. They may not have known all the words of God's law, but through grace they had become fully acquainted with the God who gave the law. There is truly "nothing between their souls and their Savior."

A couple I know hit hard financial times early on in their marriage. After falling behind on several bills, they began to receive phone calls from debt collectors and letters threatening repossession. One bill they especially wanted to keep on top of because the wife's uncle had cosigned for them. Unfortunately, things got so strained that they just could not pay it one month. After receiving a penalty notice, they contacted the company to make payment arrangements but learned that the bill was current. They praised God for the miracle, wondering what could have happened. Years later, I happened to be at a social event attended by the wife's uncle. Somehow the conversation turned to credit scores, and—without revealing details—the uncle shared that he had possessed a perfect credit score until a person he had cosigned for defaulted on the loan. When asked how he reacted, he simply replied that he paid the arrears and penalty, but never informed the person of his action.

Imagine, his niece and her husband were praising God for a miracle, but had no idea that their deliverance had come at a price. They had received grace only because somebody had met the terms of the law. God in His divine wisdom knows that the effects of Adam's sin have placed us all in arrears. If we worked all of our life, we could never pay the delinquent bill that the law requires. It is for this very reason that Christ assumed our debt and paid it off along with all interest and penalties. Now we need not fear death's debt collector, because grace has empowered us to claim ownership of the wonderful gift of life that Christ secured for us on Calvary.

---

[1] See discussion on Balaam in K. A. Burton, *The Blessing of Africa: The Bible and African Christianity*, pp. 68-70.

[2] For examples of commandments from the Book of the Dead, see Warren Matthews, *World Religions*, 6th. ed. (Belmont, Calif.: Wadsworth, 2010), p. 48.

[3] See Piotr Michalowski, "Hammurapi," in *Eerdmans Dictionary of the Bible*, pp. 545, 546.

[4] See Ellen G. White, *Prophets and Kings* (Mountain View, Calif.: Pacific Press Pub. Assn., 1917), pp. 367-378.

[5] Jennifer K. Berenson Maclean, "Lex Talionis," in *Eerdmans Dictionary of the Bible*, p. 807.

[6] Ellen G. White, *Patriarchs and Prophets* (Mountain View, Calif.: Pacific Press Pub. Assn., 1890), p. 157.

[7] E. G. White, *The Desire of Ages*, p. 638.

[8] *Ibid.*

CHAPTER 10

Christ, the Law, and the Covenants

M y parents had no idea where I was going when I left home that Sabbath afternoon. Probably I would not have told them if they had asked. All week I had been negotiating the price of a car with my cousin's boyfriend. We had finally agreed on £50, and I just could not wait another day to seal the deal. For two important reasons, we could not finalize the transaction at my parents' home. Most obvious was the question of God's law regarding doing business on the Sabbath. However, the rebellious nature of my action was also compounded by the fact that I had just turned 17 and didn't even have a driver's license! Undeterred by such details, I met Roderick at Norwood Junction, and after exchanging cash and signing the necessary papers, I drove away in a red Hillman Hunter in desperate need of a paint job. Then I parked the car so far from the house that it would be weeks before my parents discovered what I had done.

Drama has also surrounded most of my subsequent car purchases. I thought my next car, a Humber Scepter, had been abandoned on the streets of London, as were so many vehicles back then. When I encountered it, all four tires were flat, and dust and pollen covered it. Accompanied by my brother and a friend, we began to strip the car for parts, only to discover— when the owner angrily approached us—that it wasn't abandoned. After I explained myself, he named a price, and I reluctantly became the owner of two cars (by then I had secured my license). Before I left England, I had purchased two more cars (a Morris Marina and a Hillman Avenger), both of which could tell their own spectacular stories about their time with me!

After moving to Alabama, I didn't purchase my first car until my junior year of college. It was there that I first learned the term *buyer's remorse*. Based solely on the word of a friend, I gullibly forked out $500 for a car I had never seen. My stupidity was quickly manifested when, after I had picked up the Volkswagen Passat, I discovered while driving downhill that the brakes didn't work. Fortunately, it had a manual transmission, and I managed to use the gears to slow it down, barely avoiding a major catastrophe. Although I got rid of that car at my earliest opportunity, it was a case of jumping from the frying pan into the fire.

It was a rainy day when I drove into the used-car lot on Jordan Lane. My friend Junior Alexander had purchased his car here, and everything seemed to be working out well for him. I knew I did not have enough cash to purchase anything on the lot, so for the first time in my life I secured a car loan. After trading in my Volkswagen Passat and giving the salesman another $250, I was left with a $1,000 balance that I would pay back at $50 a month for two years. With my last car experience fresh on my mind, I had taken the Mazda GLC Sport for a test-drive, and the engine sounded rather quiet *in the rain*. The custom gold markings on the side and upgraded interior made me feel good about my acquisition. Once the papers were signed, I drove off the lot and headed straight to my girlfriend's dorm to show off *our* new chariot. As I pulled into the parking lot of the University of Alabama's Huntsville campus I anticipated Cynthia's exuberant response when she had the opportunity to encounter this sporty ride. I jerked out of my daydreaming when after driving over a speed bump I heard a loud thump before the car screeched to a stubborn halt and refused to respond to my attempts to restart the engine. The radiator had fallen out!

By now the sun had come out, and when I exited the car to assess the damage, I noticed that the same car that had looked so shiny *in the rain* was terribly weather-beaten. My girlfriend (who still married me after this embarrassing incident!) had already received a phone call about my new purchase and was eager to celebrate with me. Instead, we mourned as I called the dealership in a bid to reverse the transaction that had been finalized less than two hours ago. It was then that I encountered another used-car term: *as is*. From the moment I signed and drove off the lot, the car was my full responsibility, and I had to make every payment even if it was never drivable again. Having used all of my cash as part of the down payment, I had no choice but to entrust the "lemon" for repairs to the same people from whom I had purchased it. To make matters worse, I had to sign an amended contract that extended my payments for another five months!

Legally bound by the contract, I hated to make those payments. Every month that I walked into the dealer's office to honor my commitment, I relived the painful memories of that rainy day when I made a costly mistake. I am fully aware that my unfortunate experience is by no means typical. Most people who purchase a car on credit are overjoyed to know that they have a semblance of ownership even if they won't get full possession of the title until the car is completely paid for. As long as they abide by the terms of the contract, they have nothing to fear. However, if they ever face a circumstance in which they cannot meet the payments, that shiny new vehicle will get repossessed and returned to the creditor who paid for it in the first place.

Modern contracts help us to understand the ancient role of covenants, both of which fall under the general category of an agreement. By definition, an agreement involves two parties and is governed by stipulated terms. The terms of some agreements may be open for negotiation, while a dominant element may determine the rules for others. For example, a buyer is free to negotiate the final price of a house or car, but a student must pay whatever an educational institution charges. Although we can use the terms *covenant* and *contract* synonymously, a clear distinction between them contributes to their uniqueness. Whereas *contract* conjures the image of legally binding words inscribed on a document or articulated in the presence of witnesses, *covenant* focuses on the actual parties involved in the agreement—it is more relational. For the rest of the chapter we will see how God's biblical covenants portray His ultimate desire to enter into a permanent relationship with fallen humanity.

The Scope of the Covenant

Interestingly, some theologians believe that the first recorded covenant appears in Scripture before humans even transgressed God's law. They see it implicitly stated in the second chapter of Genesis when God informed Adam, "You may freely eat of every tree in the garden; but of the tree of the knowledge of good and evil you shall not eat, for in the day that you eat of it you shall die" (Gen. 2:16, 17). Although the customary Hebrew term for covenant (*berîth*) does not appear here, the passage contains the necessary elements for an agreement: it involves two parties, and it clearly states the terms.

The pattern we see in Genesis 2 is typical of all the other covenants that God makes throughout the ages. They follow the form of ancient *suzerain-vassal* treaties between a king and his subjects.[1] Notice that God does not negotiate the terms with Adam—He simply reveals the infraction and the consequences. In our postmodern world, which arrives at agreement by consensus, such an approach may seem heavy-handed. However, God's action in no way compares to the despots who use their power to extract taxes and forced labor from their underlings. His desire is not to diminish Adam but to keep him elevated. Similar to a manufacturer intimately involved with a product from the time the idea was conceived to its final assembly, God knows Adam better than the man does himself. The Lord's specific command was His way of telling him how to remain in pristine condition. Adam could enjoy the fullness of life only as long as he followed what God knew was best for him.

The first man's disobedience ushered in the era of sin that plagues us to this very day. The face-to-face communion with God that Eve and Adam experienced before the Fall should have been the ecstatic privilege of all humans. Instead, the relationship ruptured as the formerly "good" creation quickly absorbed the stench of sin and became so saturated with wickedness that God had no choice but to destroy all but a minute remnant of the creatures He had so carefully designed. Following the cleansing, God made another covenant with Noah, this time using explicit covenant language.

In reality, the one presented to Noah was not just for him, but includes *all* creation. Yahweh proclaims, "I am establishing my covenant with you and your descendants after you, and with every living creature that is with you, the birds, the domestic animals, and every animal of the earth with you, . . . and never again shall there be a flood to destroy the earth" (Gen. 9:9-11). Again we see a divine declaration not arrived at through human negotiation. We also notice that although humans directly benefit from the covenant, it places no conditions upon them. This type of covenant is akin to the type of agreement in a will, in which individuals receive a benefit simply because someone wants them to. In most cases they cannot do anything to earn or lose it. It's theirs to do with as they please.

God's covenant with Abram has elements of both a will and a contract. The initial announcement comes in the form of a promise: "I will make of you a great nation, and I will bless you, and make your name great, so that you will be a blessing. I will bless those who bless you, and the one who curses you I will curse; and in you all the families of the earth shall be blessed" (Gen. 12:2, 3). Notice that while the covenant specifically focuses on Abram's physical descendants, it also has universal implications. God is basically covenanting that Abram's descendants will play a unique role in sharing His blessings with the world. They do not need to do anything to earn their privileged status. God repeats the terms of the covenant when He changes Abram's name to Abraham (Gen. 17:1-8). However, this time He declares that those chosen to be the agents of the covenant must also bear the sign of circumcision (verses 9-14).

Heretofore, the previous covenants had involved impersonal signs. The tree of the knowledge of good and evil should have been enough to remind Adam of the relationship that God desired to have with him. Similarly, the multicolored translucency of the rainbow serves as a perpetual reminder to all that never again will a global flood decimate the earth. However, the sign for the covenant with Abraham was highly personalized and called for every male descendant of Abraham to mark himself so that he would have a daily reminder of his role in God's ultimate plan to bless all nations. When observing his circumcision, the descendant of Abraham would not only be aware of his role in transmitting Abraham's seed, but would be reminded that the love God had showered on them will ultimately be transmitted to the world. Rather than serving as a means to gain God's favor, circumcision was a reminder that the Lord had already granted Abraham's descendants favor when He included them in the terms of His covenant.

Covenant Obligations

Whimsical temperaments, political expediency, and economic realities may affect promises made by fallible human potentates. I am reminded of this whenever I return to the United Kingdom and read the script on the various denominations of bank notes. For instance, one reads: "I promise to pay the bearer on demand the sum of *ten pounds.*" Most people don't know that the wording goes back to a time that you could exchange the note for silver, a pound of which weighed 240 silver pennies. The currency itself served as a promissory note, and the Bank of England was obligated to turn over 2,400 silver pennies for anyone issued a 10-pound note. Of course, if you entered a British bank today and demanded to exchange paper money for silver coins, you would either be laughed at or escorted out! Although the money is still legal tender, the change from a *commodity-* to a *fiat*-based economy means that the promissory statement is null and void. Economic realities make it impossible for the Bank of England to live up to its end of the covenant.

Fortunately, politics or transient economies do not influence God's covenants. When He establishes a covenant, He commits Himself to abide by it. History has already demonstrated His fidelity. While countless localized floods have swept over the landscape, never again has one devastated the entire inhabited world. Further, in fulfillment of the terms in His covenant with Abraham, his physical descendants did indeed inhabit the land of Canaan. In fact, God has demonstrated how serious He is in living up to His covenant promises by offering His one and only Son as the culminating seed of Abraham who mystically encapsulates the entire human race (see Gal. 3:15-29). Christ's death and resurrection has secured our glorious future as we await the new heavens and earth, where the capital will be located on the New Canaan in the New Jerusalem!

Since a covenant involves two parties, it stands to reason that it would have obligations on both sides. For instance, in return for public services rendered, governments require citizens to pay taxes, or those who win the lottery must sign a document to confirm their decision to take a lump-sum payout or receive regular installments. In His covenant with humanity God has chosen to reveal the details incrementally. He first expresses His desire for a relationship by promising never to destroy the earth again by floodwaters. Then He selects Abraham's family to be His ambassadors of hope. It will take decades after the divine appointment of Abraham's progeny before God announces the circumcision requirement.

Given the devious intentions of some in the power position of a contract, we tend to be wary of agreements in which certain details show up only after the subordinate party has signed the document. "Small print" has been the bane of many who find themselves trapped in disadvantageous deals that they are legally obligated to honor. Here in the United States hundreds of thousands of students experience such frustration when repayment of government-endorsed student loans shocks them into learning the difference between simple and compounded interest. The very entities that promised to ease the financial burden of receiving an education quickly turn into manipulative institutions intent on keeping them in long-term indebtedness.

God's covenant with humanity does not contain deceitful small print or ambiguous conditions. The very fact that that He has taken millennia to share the details is enough to establish His desire for everyone to understand the terms.[2] Abraham's male descendants underwent the rite of circumcision for centuries before God revealed the details of the law of love upon which He based the covenant. Every detail of the ten-commandment law was known to the Israelites long before God systematically codified it and engraved it in stone by His very finger. Not desiring to trick us into covenanting with Him, He rather wants us to relate to Him with our full consciousness. As to adhering to the covenantal legal requirements, ours is an obligation of *choice*, not force.

It is important to remember that those who willingly choose to remain in a covenant relationship with God don't have the option to reject His law. As we have stated numerous times before, they don't observe His law to *gain* His favor but follow His commandments because they already *have* it. They deem it as a privilege, not a punishment. The truth is, only those with a correct view of God are capable of truly observing His law. They see God as a *doctor* rather than a *dictator*. A dictator possesses an unbending philosophy easily encapsulated in the dictum "my way or the highway." However, God is not the malevolent dictator but the benevolent doctor. He knows that the transition from sin to righteousness involved a radically lifesaving surgery. Now, in order for His patients to *experience* healing, they must adapt to a new regimen. God's new prescription for their lives may take some getting used to, but they know it's for their good, so they follow the Doctor's orders. If they don't, then the operation has been in vain. They will be like the person who undergoes bariatric surgery without rejecting an unhealthy lifestyle, only to see the pounds return months later.

The consequences for living outside of the divine covenant relationship may seem like direct divine punishment, but they are basically self-inflicted. God's covenant with humans is really His articulated desire to guard us from the unbridled terrors of satanic wickedness. One who chooses to be in covenant relation with the Lord steps into a protective circle in which the enemy of souls is utterly powerless. Those who violate the relationship often get enticed by the seemingly greener grass outside the parameters of the circle, only to find out that the view up close is not as enticing as the one from a distance. Like Adam, we've all bitten into the aromatic and attractive fruit, only to discover that rancidity and rot reside under the deceptively alluring skin. All in all, the choice is ours, and only we can decide how we will respond to Joshua's appeal: "Choose this day whom you will serve" (Joshua 24:15).

The Covenant Life

Thanks to the saving grace of Jesus, all who choose to serve God can start enjoying the fruit of the covenant immediately. In a strange but real way, we experience the opposite of what Adam and Eve faced after they ate the forbidden fruit. God warned Adam that death would come on the *very day* in which he disobeyed (Gen. 2:17). Someone first encountering the text would probably wonder why death did not consume Adam immediately after his infraction. However, it is important that we allow the Bible to interpret itself. God said that death would result from rebellion, and the Bible records, "Thus all the days that Adam lived were nine hundred thirty years; *and he died*" (Gen. 5:5). The process of death was slow and probably started on a micro level as Adam and Eve experienced biological deterioration. But eventually all of their organs would cease to function, and the life lent to them by the Giver would return to Him.

An understanding of the process of original death helps us to understand the phases of eternal life. In both instances we catch glimpses of God's matchless grace. I'm sure He could have arranged it so that the forbidden fruit would be the trigger to a high-powered sniper's rifle aimed directly at the target's heart. However, He chose to leave His life source with Adam even after the man chose to break the covenant with Him. Death would eventually come, but not before Adam discovered God's ultimate plan to reconcile Himself to His beloved creation. Similarly, when those affected and infected by sin choose to become covenant partners with Him, He immediately commutes the death sentence and the sinner begins to experience eternal life.

The sinner is like the beach-stranded starfish, destined for certain death if it does not return to the water. Unable to make the journey in its own strength, it is rescued by a passerby who picks it up and hurls it back into the sea. John may have had a similar picture in mind when he declared, "Very truly, I tell you, anyone who hears my word and believes him who sent me has eternal life, and does not come under judgment, but has passed from death to life" (John 5:24). We see the urgent imagery behind the disciple's words revealed in a precise translation of the last clause, which literally states that the believer "has already been *thrown* from death to life"! Consequently, believers live in a seeming paradox as they face the vicissitudes of life while resting in the assurance of salvation (see Eph. 2:6).

Everyone who has embraced the divine restoration embedded in the covenants will choose to live by kingdom principles. In our age of superheroes in which comic-book characters are the subjects of Hollywood blockbusters, some Christian ministers suggest that kingdom people possess supernatural abilities and wealth. However, while those in a covenant relationship with God will definitely receive spiritual gifts, the sign of true citizenship is love-driven obedience (John 13:34, 35). In his famous "love chapter" Paul clearly indicates that it is possible for people to manifest "spiritual" actions outside of a divine context (1 Cor. 13). God may not have granted a kingdom person the gift of healing, exorcising, or preaching, but they will display the indispensable trait of love.

Indeed, the law of the covenant, summarized in the Ten Commandments, serves to remind us of the kingdom principles that will guide us for eternity. Those who live by them will be forever mindful of their covenant obligations in all of their relationships. God alone will be the aim of their worship; and their love for Him is so strong that not even family, friends, pastor, or denomination can come between them and the object of their devotion. They will understand the meaning of true commitment and will not be complacent with merely belonging to a church that *teaches* truth but fails to *practice* love. As they learn to love their Savior, the "things of earth will grow strangely dim" as their time with Him extends way beyond their weekly Sabbath appointments.

Those in a covenant relationship with God will also exhibit love in their relationships with other humans. Spouses will truly search for ways to find happiness *in* their marriages and not look outside for temporary thrills to satisfy sinful impulses. Parents will view themselves as patient guardians of the children whom God has entrusted to their care, and children will see them as effective reflections of their *true* Parent. Victims of hurt and betrayal may have to appeal for justice, but they will not seek retributive vengeance on their perpetrators. Employers will not view their employees and customers as expendable commodities whose sole purpose is to increase their net worth. Church members will not be so caught up in acquiring *things* for themselves that they fail to see the millions who so desperately *need* the things that we *want*.

I will be the first to admit that it's not always easy to abide by kingdom principles. Years of selfish habits make it difficult for some of us to do naturally what is unnatural to our spirit. Nonetheless, we cannot afford to allow our passions to dictate our decisions. If we are serious about our covenant relationship with God, we will surrender our will to His and experience the transformation that comes through the renewing of our minds (Rom. 12:1, 2). Slowly but surely we will realize the fulfillment of God's covenant promise: "I will put my law within them, and I will write it on their hearts; and I will be their God, and they shall be my people" (Jer. 31:33).

Conclusion
Even before the advent of sin God desired a lifelong relationship with

the jewels of His creation. While Satan constantly seeks to thwart His plans, God is determined to restore humans one day to full communion with Him. So committed is He to this end, that He has entered into an unbreakable covenant with the human race. He incrementally revealed its terms through Noah, Abraham, Moses, and ultimately Christ. Although each revelatory phase provides new information, the essence of the covenant remains the same: God *will* restore His relationship with humanity.

Since we are His covenant partners, God requests that we be as committed to Him as He has been to us. He has demonstrated that pledge by granting us an eternal happiness that none of us deserve or could even earn. All He asks in return is that we express our appreciation by yielding to His Spirit so that He can impute the life of His Son to us. Of course, it calls for our cooperation as we learn to submit our stubborn wills to Him. God is so vested in our success that He has revealed His law of love to aid us in the decision-making process. That same law will be inscribed on our hearts for eternity.

After years of driving preowned cars, my new bride and I walked into the Hyundai showroom in Skokie, Illinois, and after intense negotiations walked out as the proud owners of a brand-new charcoal-gray 1989 Sonata. In reality the General Motors Acceptance Corporation was the real owner, but for all intents and purposes it was *our* car—as long as we made the monthly payment. We encountered some serious economic times, and some months I wondered if the finance company would take possession of it. Nonetheless, we were able to satisfy our commitments and rejoiced when after 36 months of payments we finally received the title to *our* car.

When Jesus died on Calvary's cross, He paid the full price for eternal life for all humanity. We don't have to wait until we have done enough good things to get it—we can claim it immediately. Sadly, some refuse to accept the gift, choosing instead to live a selfish life governed by impulse. However, those who truly appreciate what God has done will enter into covenant relationship with Him, as they govern their lives according to the kingdom principles outlined in His law of love.

---

[1] For a discussion on the unique characteristics of biblical suzerain covenants, see P. J. Achtemeier, ed., *Harpers's Bible Dictionary*, 1st ed. (San Francisco: Harper and Row, 1985), pp. 191, 192.

[2] O. Palmer Robertson speaks of the "continuity" of the covenants in *The Christ of the Covenants* (Phillipsburg, N.J.: P & R Publishing, 1981), p. 281.

CHAPTER 11

Christ's Apostles and the Law

During a recent discussion on Christian living, a student lamented about how the church was demonstrating signs of apostasy. His basic issue involved the General Conference's "decision" to lift the ban on wedding rings. I had to admit to him that I had never heard of such a decision nor was I aware of the ban. When I asked him for the source of the information, it did not at all surprise me when he provided the name of a popular speaker whose conspiracy theories are especially attractive to the inquiring minds of our young people. But it's not just the young. I recently visited a church in which a very mature leader shared with the stunned congregation the "breaking news" of the Papacy's lawsuit against the Adventist Church for *The Great Controversy* distribution initiative. His source? The Internet!

I'm not sure what it is about human nature, but when a person of influence declares something with authority, few take the time to research the facts. An uncritical tendency to trust authority figures has been the source of much division and contention in the church. Unfortunately, the problem probably derives from catechistic teaching methods in which we tell our youth *what* to believe but do not give them the freedom to examine *why*. Such a system may seem easier to manage because those imparting knowledge can do so without being challenged or interrupted, but it robs the student of the God-given gift of discovery. Perhaps that is why Ellen G. White counsels that we should train our youth as "thinkers, and not mere reflectors of other [people's] thoughts."[1]

I will be the first to admit that the "groupthink" virus has also afflicted me. I still remember in my teenage years being mesmerized by an evangelist's fancy charts and slides and listening intently as he lowered his voice to share a dangerous secret. Slowly looking over both shoulders before leaning toward us, he whispered, "In the Vatican right now the pope has a miter inscribed with the words *Vicarius Filii Dei!*" The familiar click of the slide-changing carousel drew our attention to the screen, on which we viewed an "actual" picture of *the* miter emblazoned with the letters that collectively had a numerical value of 666. When the Spirit called me to ministry, I couldn't wait for my first opportunity to share this secret in a sermon, and did so with gusto on many occasions. I can't describe to you how befuddled I felt when I discovered that the miter story was an Adventist "urban legend." Needless to say, I immediately changed my sermon notes!

Another summons to preaching with integrity occurred at a kosher Jewish restaurant in Skokie, Illinois. My doctoral advisor, Robert Jewett, had invited me to join him for lunch with a noted theologian from the University of Tel Aviv. Our guest was a Conservative Jew who had shared his discomfort at seeing Jewish houses of worship that took the name "temple" rather than "synagogue." As far as this pious Jew was concerned, there could be only one Temple. That was why it shocked me when he announced his order to the waiter. *Duck?* I screamed internally. *Isn't this a kosher restaurant?* Unable to contain my shock, I asked, "They serve *duck* here?" My guest humored me with a nod, but probably wondered why I was so confounded. I felt the need to give my Jewish friend a Bible study from the Torah, but my better sense told me to keep quiet. That very evening when I returned to my apartment I frantically—then patiently—searched the Bible and reference books for the "webbed feet" forbidden food list I had heard about (and preached about) for years. Although I'm not suggesting that we should go out and start eating ducks (or flying locusts, for that matter), I'm still looking for the text!

Perhaps my most shocking discovery was finding out that some Christians began observing Sunday before the edict of Constantine in the year A.D. 321. When I first heard that Constantine was the one responsible for "changing the day of worship," I shared those "irrefutable" facts whenever I got an opportunity. How could anyone dispute the historical record? As far as I was concerned, it was he who had disturbed the three-century tradition of Christian Sabbathkeeping. Ironically, while such a teaching has been most effective in convicting an untold number of people about the Sabbath *truth*, it is not grounded in historical *truth*. While as emperor Constantine did pass a law that "all townspeople should rest on the venerable day of the sun," many Christians had been advocating Sunday over Sabbath since the second century.[2]

Truth should matter for followers of Christ. How can anyone trust us when we offer the Bible as a guide for righteous living yet distort facts for the sake of baptisms? Christ calls us to be "wise as serpents," but does the "end justify the means" if the means are laden with values that contradict the end? I'm sure that many who continue to convey common Adventist legends do so with sincerity. After all, most myths contain elements of truth. Apparently, although it does not appear on a miter, *Vicarius Filii Dei* has been used to designate the pope; Constantine did play an instrumental role in popularizing Sunday observance; and it is not hard to see how a person can transfer ungulate "cloven hoof" imagery to avian feet. However, we misrepresent God when we use such ideas to trick people into making spiritual decisions, especially when we hold others accountable for the way in which their denominations have misrepresented the biblical teaching about the law. For the rest of this chapter we will respond to the oft-repeated charge that Christ's apostles taught that it is no longer necessary to observe the law.

Christ's Theologian and the Law

Much of the fodder from which the opponents of God's law construct their straw man comes from the writings of the apostle Paul. Isolating certain texts from their literary, cultural, and historical contexts, countless Bible scholars have reinvented a Paul who would not be recognized in his world. Their Paul is so repulsed by the Judaism he had been once prepared to kill and die for, that he exchanged a radical legalism for a relaxed libertarianism. In her practical book on the house churches in Romans, my dear friend Reta Halteman-Finger even has Paul endorsing the consumption of pork for non-Jewish believers in the early church![3] The fact that non-Adventists currently reading this book would probably be surprised at the exclamation at the end of the previous sentence is proof of the successful reinvention of Paul.

Some of my friends who proclaim Paul's disdain for the law believe that their position is rooted in biblical authority. I would be the first to admit that the way some present it makes their evidence seem strong. The book of Romans alone has several texts that one could use to build what might seem a compelling case. Take, for instance, Paul's statement in his discussion about genuine righteousness: "For we hold that a person is justified by faith apart from works prescribed by the law" (Rom. 3:28). And at the end of his discourse on the meaning of the death and resurrection of Christ for the Christian he declares, "For sin will have no dominion over you, since you are not under law but under grace" (Rom. 6:14). Further, those looking for a knockout punch can easily refer to the famous marriage analogy in which the apostle clearly states, "You have died to the law through the body of Christ" (Rom. 7:4).

For some, these texts would be enough to close the case, but others cite additional texts. For instance, in one of his discussions on the law in Galatians, Paul concludes, "Therefore the law was our disciplinarian until Christ came, so that we might be justified by faith. But now that faith has come, we are no longer subject to a disciplinarian" (Gal. 3:24, 25). Then there is the somewhat obscure text from Colossians often employed as a basis to reject the fourth commandment of God's law. Here Paul admonishes: "Do not let anyone condemn you in matters of food and drink or of observing festivals, new moons, or *sabbaths*. These are only a shadow of what is to come, but the substance belongs to Christ" (Col. 2:16, 17). Although the previous texts might appear to build an effective case, if I were the prosecuting attorney, here is the one I would reserve for the last: "He has abolished the law with its commandments and ordinances, that he might create in himself one new humanity in place of the two, thus making peace" (Eph. 2:15).

If presented to a neutral jury, it is hard to see how the prosecution could lose. With such a barrage of biblical texts to support the argument, how could anyone dispute the charge that Christians no longer have any obligation to keep the ten-commandment law? Indeed, hundreds of millions of Christians over the ages have followed this argument to its logical conclusion and opted for a hybrid religion that would be foreign to the earliest believers in Jesus as Savior and Messiah. Nonetheless, as compelling as the evidence for the prosecution might seem, before the jury presents its final verdict, it would be prudent to heed the warning contained in Proverbs: "The one who first states a case seems right, until the other comes and cross-examines" (Prov. 18:17).

The Bible does not need a shrewd lawyer who cherry-picks evidence to come to its defense. As impressive as the opponents' argument may seem, we can easily refute the class action suit against the validity of the law when we view each of the texts in their contexts. For instance, while Paul did say that it is faith and not law that justifies a person, two verses later he asks (and answers): "Do we then overthrow the law by this faith? By no means! On the contrary, we uphold the law" (Rom. 3:31). He uses a similar formula after confirming that we are not under law but grace: "What then? Should we sin because we are not under law but under grace? By no means!" (Rom. 6:15). Then he employs the same rhetorical device after his declaration that believers have died to the law: "What then should we say? That the law is sin? By no means! . . . [On the contrary] the law is holy, and the commandment is holy and just and good" (Rom. 7:7-12).

For those who believe in the unity of scriptural doctrine, this should be enough to dismiss the case as frivolous. However, untold members of the jury indoctrinated into a certain way of thinking for many years will not be satisfied until we have explained the other pieces of evidence. The text in Galatians also has an overarching context. Just before Paul speaks of the law as a "disciplinarian" he lends his support for the law in the same characteristic question-response style that we see in Romans: "Is the law then opposed to the promises of God? Certainly not! For if a law had been given that could make alive, then righteousness would indeed come through the law" (Gal. 3:21). We would need a lot more space to provide a context for the Colossians text, but the key to understanding it is in the admonition ("do not let anyone condemn you" [Col. 2:16]) and the explanation ("these *are* only a shadow of what is to come" [verse 17]). In all likelihood we have here a similar context to the one Paul addresses in Romans 14, in which he asks Gentile Christians to be tolerant toward the cultural practices of Jewish Christians and vice versa. As such, the law *implied* in the discussion (notice that the term *law* does not even appear) more than likely refers to the cultural Jewish ceremonies.

Our brief analysis of the passage in Colossians is a firm reminder that an understanding of the sociocultural context of the text can be just as important as comprehending the literary context. Such an observation is key to understanding the prosecution's "linchpin" text from Ephesians. A superficial reading can easily have a person stuck on Paul's words: "He has abolished the law" (Eph. 2:15). However, if that were Paul's intended meaning, is he saying that it's now OK to steal, kill, commit adultery, and covet? As we have seen in a number of passages, Paul himself would emphatically declare, "By no means!" So how are we to understand a seemingly contradictory text that some have used to eclipse all of his other statements about the law? Here again, the text itself provides the context for understanding.

Paul here addresses the issue of Gentile "inclusion" into the Sinai covenant. Heretofore, it was their uncircumcised status and prohibition from participating in the Temple services that caused their "exclusion." A literal "dividing wall" (verse 14) that stood in the Temple at the very time that Paul wrote to the saints in Ephesus symbolized that prohibition. It meant that Gentile believers could never participate in the Temple ceremonies. Indeed, it was to the ceremonial laws that Paul refers in verse 15, which literally reads "the law of commandments with teachings"; or more loosely, "the part of the law that contains specific doctrines" *(ton nomon tōn entolōn en dogmasin)*. The apostle wants the Ephesians to know that no physical or doctrinal obstacle can ever block their access to the Father (verses 17, 18). Rather than proclaiming the nullification of the law of love, he invites them into the covenant circle where they can join the descendants of Abraham and Israel in discovering the peace that comes to those who love God's law.

Christ's Inner Circle and the Law

The apostle Peter, a contemporary of Paul, noted that contentious expositors had utilized the latter's philosophized theological approach as fodder for their divisive teaching since the fledgling days of the Jesus movement. He writes, "There are some things [in Paul's teachings that are] hard to understand, which the ignorant and unstable twist to their own destruction, as they do the other scriptures" (2 Peter 3:16). The words that follow are telling: "You therefore, beloved, since you are forewarned, beware that you are not carried away with the error of the *lawless* and lose your own stability" (verse 17). Based on Peter's warning, it is not difficult to see that some false teachers used Paul to justify their antilaw positions. As far as he is concerned, their actions are no different from the lawless *(athesmōn)* reprobates who resided in Sodom during Lot's era (2 Peter 2:7).

If any of Jesus' disciples would have insight into any intention He may have had to abolish the law, it would have been Peter. Together with the brothers James and John, he formed a part of Christ's inner circle that shared some of His most intimate moments. It was he among the disciples who first publicly declared his belief that Jesus was indeed the Christ of prophecy (Matt. 16:16), and it was to him that Jesus gave a special charge after the Resurrection (John 21:15-19). Thus it is hard to imagine that someone so close to Jesus would not have written anything on the abrogation of the law if that was what Jesus intended.

Instead, Peter's life and teachings demonstrate his commitment to God's covenant law. An interesting example of the disciple's fidelity to biblical law appears in the book of Acts when he received a vision that appeared to be nullifying the law regarding clean and unclean foods (Acts 10:1-16).

The incident took place about five years after Christ had ascended into heaven. By then, Peter had experienced great numerical success in his preaching ministry, and we find nothing to indicate that the content of his preaching was antilaw in any way. In fact, his commitment to the law is the very reason that the vision and the divine command to kill and eat the forbidden food shocked him. If Christ had declared the Ten Commandments null and void, what would be the justification for Peter's continued adherence to a seemingly "lesser" law?

Although his attitude to the law before the vision is clear, we might still argue that the vision provided new light on the law. In a sense, this is true, but only as it relates to the truth of Gentile inclusion that Paul so eloquently expounds in Ephesians 2. We see this indisputably clarified in the text when Peter explains that God gave him the vision to show him that he "should not call *anyone* profane or unclean" (Acts 10:28). It was all about his need to love all people and had nothing to do with the validity of the law. When he did speak about the law, he reminded followers of Christ to "abstain from the desires of the flesh that wage war against the soul" (1 Peter 2:11). Interestingly, his admonition appears immediately after he addresses his audience with the same covenant language that God entrusted to Israel at Sinai: "You are a chosen race, a royal priesthood, a holy nation, God's own people" (verse 9; cf. Ex. 19:6). Just as with their spiritual forebears, God expects the body of Christ to reflect the principles of His loving covenant law in their relationships.

Nowhere do we see the loving nature of God's law more manifest in the New Testament than in the writings of John. Another member of Jesus' inner circle, the disciple was privy to many things about Him that are not included in his writings (John 21:25). Since he obviously selected what to include, it only stands to reason that the matters he wrote about were those he deemed important. It is no accident, then, that in all of the literature attributed to him, John writes about the necessity of commandment keeping for those who profess to be in relationship with God. He has Jesus Himself testify about the inseparable link between love and obedience: "If you keep my commandments, you will abide in my love, just as I have kept my Father's commandments and abide in his love" (John 15:10).

A person looking to split hairs could easily interpret Jesus' words to indicate a difference between His commandments and His Father's. Although we have already discussed this objection in a previous chapter, it wouldn't hurt to reemphasize the fact that the Son and the Father's commandments are one and the same. They are both guidelines for love. Hence, in his First Epistle, John writes, "Now by this we may be sure that we know him, if we obey his commandments. . . . Whoever obeys his word, truly in this person the love of God has reached perfection" (1 John 2:3-5). Elsewhere he remarks, "This is love, that we walk according to his commandments" (2 John 6). As far as John is concerned, loving obedience is the only mark of God's genuine child (3 John 11).

According to John's testimony, fidelity to God's commandments was not just an obligation for the first generation of believers, but for followers of Christ in all ages. In his final prophetic utterance, which originated from the very mind of God (Rev. 1:1), he informs us that God's last-day saints will "keep the commandments of God and hold fast to the faith of Jesus" (Rev. 14:12). They realize that they are saved solely by the faithfulness of Jesus, who perfectly kept His Father's law. However, they are also sensitive to the fact that although they can never repay such a matchless act of love, if they choose to accept the gift of salvation, they will lovingly model God's kingdom principles by ordering their actions in conformity to His law. Perhaps it is in recognition of our loving obligation that some Bible manuscripts render John's (and the Bible's) final beatitude with the words "Blessed are those who keep His commandments, that they may have a right to the tree of life and may enter through the gates into the city" (see Rev. 22:14).

Christ's Brothers and the Law

The James who wrote the New Testament Epistle would have been the first to resound the "amen" to John's final beatitude. His teaching on the law of love is so succinct and clear that those who practice a selective reading charge him with being at odds with Christ's theologian, Paul. The clarity of James's teaching so disturbed Protestant Reformer Martin Luther that in an early version of his Bible translation he referred to James's letter as "the epistle of straw" (omitted in later editions). Beguiled by the seeming dichotomy, critical scholars of the nineteenth century concocted an elaborate drama of warring factions in the early church: a "grace" party headed by Paul and a "law" party under the leadership of James.

While such proof-text and conspiratorial-influenced scholarship makes interesting reading and has captured the imagination of an untold number of biblical scholars, an objective examination of the biblical witness cannot support it. In fact, James's teaching on the law could very well serve as a preface to, or summary of, Paul's. The two were by no means strangers, and probably met on several occasions. While we find three notable people named James in the New Testament, it is generally believed that the one who wrote the Epistle was Jesus' brother (Matt. 13:55). If Jesus had wanted to abolish the law, surely He would have informed His sibling.

Rather than calling for an end to the law, James argues for its authority. In fact, his candid exposition graphically portrays how lawkeeping in a loving manner actually looks.[4] Speaking to the gulf between the rich and the poor in his community, he writes, "You do well if you really fulfill the royal law according to the scripture, 'You shall love your neighbor as yourself.' But if you show partiality, you commit sin and are convicted by the law as transgressors" (James 2:8, 9). Those who are genuine about their covenant relationship will allow the law to inform their decisions about how to relate to others. They don't arbitrarily select which precepts of the law to follow while neglecting others. After all, what is the benefit of honoring the Sabbath if our hearts have not been sensitized to the suffering around us? Why covet that new vehicle we *can* afford, when there are members in our congregation who are struggling to make ends meet? And why pray for some person when God has enabled you to be the answer to that individual's own prayer? James asks, "What good is it . . . if you say you have faith but do not have works? Can faith save you? If a brother or sister is naked and lacks daily food, and one of you says to them, 'Go in peace, keep warm and eat your fill,' and yet you do not supply their bodily needs, what is the good of that?" (verses 14-16).

James understands the inseparable link between observing the law in a loving manner and genuine faith. Authentic faith is not an esoteric creedal formula to which all believers should grant assent. The devil has done a grand job of distracting professed followers of Christ who are so fixated on doctrinal *purity* that they have no concern about the "*pure* and undefiled" religion that focuses on the heart (James 1:27). Please don't misunderstand me. A correct understanding of biblical doctrine is important, but only so far as it draws us into God's will. A person can *believe* everything the church teaches and still be on the highway to hell. James taunts, "You believe that God is one; you do well. Even the demons believe—and shudder" (James 2:19).

Ultimately, God will not judge us on what we *believe* but how we *behave*. Before anyone misinterprets my statement, let me remind you that we can do nothing to earn salvation. However, our fruit will confirm if we have accepted the offer of salvation. Saved individuals will intentionally yield to the transforming grace of God and allow the Spirit to control their choices. They do not use the law as a strategic playbook to get ahead in the race for perfection, but embrace it as a manual for learning how to conduct loving relationships. Furthermore, they understand that on the judgment day God will assess them in the same way in which they have done others. Hence James's warning: "For judgment will be without mercy to anyone who has shown no mercy; mercy triumphs over judgment" (verse 13). A person who truly keeps the law will be known for acts of mercy rather than self-righteous criticism of others' deficiencies (James 4:11, 12).

Jude's letter also takes up the theme of mercy in the context of obedience (Jude 2, 21, 22). It is generally believed that Jude is another of Jesus' four brothers (Matt. 13:55). Like James, he would have known if Jesus had released believers from an obligation to the law. However, his brief missive chiefly warns his readers about the dreadful fate of the disobedient (Jude 5-16). In fact, the reason he wrote in the first place was to counter "intruders . . . who pervert the grace of our God into licentiousness and deny our only Master and Lord, Jesus Christ" (Jude 4). Although he does not directly refer to God's law in the letter, the reference to licentiousness is proof enough that fidelity to the law is the central metanarrative. God's grace does not provide an excuse to ignore His law, and those who choose the path of selfish rebellion will receive the wrath of God in the judgment.

Fully cognizant of the fact that the gospel is a message of hope, not fear, Jude ends his letter with strong words of encouragement. He exhorts believers to render spiritual support to one another as they graciously extend mercy to those siblings who still struggle in their spiritual journey (Jude 22, 23). His final benediction points to the secret of experiencing a successful covenant relationship: "Now to him who is able to keep you from falling, and to make you stand without blemish in the presence of his glory with rejoicing, to the only God our Savior, through Jesus Christ our Lord, be glory, majesty, power, and authority, before all time and now and forever. Amen" (Jude 24, 25).

Conclusion

Christ's apostles are united in their teaching about the role of the law in the life of the believer. Some have misrepresented and maligned Paul, the most intellectual contributor to the New Testament, by seeking to portray him as an antilaw libertarian. However, those who paint him in such a negative light can make a case only by isolating certain texts from their literary, historical, and cultural contexts. When viewed in totality, it is clear that although Paul had a tendency to be philosophical in his explanations, he was a grace-filled law observer who understood that God never meant the law to be an instrument of salvation, but a manual for living.

Peter and John, members of Jesus' inner circle, heralded the same message. Knowing that believers under the new covenant had the same obligation as those to whom God had originally revealed the covenant, they emphasized the essential role of the law in governing behavior. Jesus' brothers, James and Jude, are in full harmony with their fellow apostles as they stress the mercy that must fill the hearts and actions of those who abide by the principles of God's law. Only those who understand grace can really know what it means to keep the law. Fortunately, the New Testament witness provides the necessary material for us to comprehend it.

Perhaps my biggest regret in ministry is being lured into a public debate on the Sabbath question with a prominent Church of Christ minister. When he first approached my senior pastor and me, we felt a little uncomfortable with the term *debate* and told him that we would rather have an open discussion. We left it up to him to arrange the details, and after learning the rules of the "discussion" we realized that we were indeed involved in a debate! Still we decided to go ahead, and according to the rules, he ended up having the last word. It seems as if he had been playing "rope a dope" until that point, and to our amazement he pulled out an arsenal of out-of-context proof texts that appeared to make a strong case for the transfer of the Sabbath to the first day of the week. Since we had agreed to the rules, we had no choice but to sit and listen to his distortions, all the time wishing that we could have one more round to set the record straight.

I learned my lesson the hard way. Truth is not subject to debate. Skilled debaters know how to make the audience see what they want them to, and may even trick their opponents into doubting their own position. In reality, debates are hardly ever about truth, but are geared to place the spotlight on the debater. I propose that the spirit of debate has kept the antilaw position alive, because church leaders and theologians are more concerned about defending a position than discovering truth. But when those defenses come down, the truth of God's Word will shine through, and sincere Christian men and women will come to realize that "the law is holy, and the commandment is holy and just and good" (Rom. 7:12).

---

[1] Ellen G. White, *Education* (Mountain View, Calif.: Pacific Press Pub. Assn., 1903), p. 17.

[2] See Samuele Bacchiocchi, "The Rise of Sunday Observance in Early Christianity," and Kenneth A. Strand, "The 'Lord's Day' in the Second Century," in K. A. Strand, ed., *The Sabbath in Scripture and History*, pp. 132-150, 346-351.

[3] Reta Halteman-Finger, *Paul and the Roman House Churches* (Scottdale, Pa.: Herald Press, 1991).

[4] For a concise discussion on the social issues in James, see Pedrito U. Maynard-Reid, *Poverty and Wealth in James* (Maryknoll, N.Y.: Orbis, 1987).

CHAPTER 12

Christ's Church and the Law

I am a middle child. To be more precise, I am the sixth of 10 children. Large families were an anomaly in the part of the world in which I grew up. With the rising popularity of birth control, families in England were getting smaller, and the majority of my friends had only two or three people to call brother or sister. Being raised in a three-bedroom home with only one toilet and bathroom had its challenges. I didn't know what it was to sleep alone until my parents purchased bunk beds in my teenage years. But coming from a large family also had its benefits, chief of which was always having someone to socialize with. My natural clique was my brother Peter and cousin Junior. We were each a year apart and knew exactly where to find mischief.

Although we had plenty of people to play with at home, we also had our own outside associations that we fondly called "gangs" (before the term took on a negative connotation). They were the guys we hung out with at church or school. We were usually in the same age range and had hobbies or interests in common not necessarily shared by our siblings. If my memory serves me correctly, I even did what was necessary to become a "blood brother" with a couple of my buddies (we substituted the knife with a safety pin!). During my teen years my associates and I were earning enough money to express our shared identity. Every Sunday we would put on our padded blue overalls, place a copious amount of gel in our slick-backed hair, sling our Bauer Turbo skates over our shoulders, and head to the ice-skating rink in Streatham, uniformly dressed and full of confidence. There was nothing we couldn't do.

After a while our skating group disintegrated as we chose different paths in life. By now I had a full-time job and a girlfriend and did not have as much time to "hang out" with the guys on the weekends. During my lunch breaks I formed a new association with four work colleagues who frequented Ray's Gym, the home of the Mighty Matchsticks. I couldn't wait for the 12:00 lunchtime to come so that I could clock out, walk to the corner deli for a tasty cheese, tomato, and onion crusty roll, and head to Ray's while consuming my healthy dose of carbohydrates and protein. Once there, we quickly changed into our training gear and enjoyed 35 vein-busting minutes of serious power lifting. My knees are still paying the price for those deep squats I was able to do only after tricking my smelling-salts-possessed body to push twice my body weight!

About the same time as my gym years, I was also attracted to the music scene. I had taught myself to play the bass guitar and had the privilege of being a member of a band (one of the early singers later signed a deal with a major label). My love for the bass and an awakened awareness of my Caribbean roots also compelled me to associate with a "sound system." Reflecting the social consciousness among Black youth in London at the time, the sound system was initially named "Jah Satta," before Roger (the founder) decided that "Chapter One" was more appealing. My parents weren't too pleased about it, but I would spend hours with my sound-system friends listening to the latest reggae releases and creating rhymes to instrumental versions of the hits. On Saturday nights I would help the crew to set up the huge speakers in halls or houses, and would often be at the controls with Roger, who was like a brother to me.

Although I loved the music scene, I wasn't too comfortable with some of the other things that came along with it, and soon found myself responding to the Spirit's call to ministry. It led me across the Atlantic to Huntsville, Alabama, where I made new associations. It did not take me long to get involved with the International Student Organization and the United Students' Movement. However, perhaps my most cherished relationships were with those whose names frequently appeared alongside mine on the dean's list each quarter. A healthy competition existed among us, and we rejoiced at each other's achievements.

As I transitioned from student to professional life, I found myself less drawn to social groups. Every now and then I would enjoy a game of dominoes or volleyball with friends, but without any regular commitment. My group interactions came about by virtue of my positions. For instance, the academic societies to which I belong are focused on the goals of research and publishing. Even my ministerial ordination, which grants me access into an international fraternity, is a natural consequence of my vocation.

As I reflected on the various group associations I'd had over the years, I thought about what made them meaningful. They'd all had different configurations and distinctly unique purposes, but each had had something that bound the adherents together. Whether it was the closeness in age to my siblings and schoolmates; the love of skating, music, or weight lifting; the shared immigrant experience of foreigners in a strange land; or the privilege of being numbered among successful academics or clergy, all group members had had common interests. Each entity had also had a set of rules that were either spoken or unspoken. Failure to adhere to such rules could mean the rescinding of ordination, ejection from the band, shunning from friends, or any number of negative consequences. In this chapter we will briefly survey one of the largest associations in history as we examine the central role that God's law of love has played in helping to hold the church together.

From the Tree to the Promise

I am using the term *church* to refer to God's covenant people throughout the ages. The English word for church derives from the Greek adjective *kuriakē*, which basically means "pertaining to the Lord." Interestingly, while the New Testament utilizes the adjective to refer to a "Lord's day" and "Lord's Supper" (Rev. 1:10; 1 Cor. 11:20, NIV), it never designates the Lord's people. The Greek word most often translated "church" is *ekklēsia*, a literal translation of which is "call out of," but in its original setting referred to an "assembly." People who assembled together for a specific purpose—whether secular or religious—comprised the *ekklēsia*. The "assembly" imagery suggests that God's people are not at all insignificant, but comprise a great multitude of the faithful who have chosen to remain in covenant relationship with Him (Rev. 7:9).

As we discussed in a previous chapter, the foundation of the church goes back to the very beginning when God presented Adam with a test of loyalty. Apparently it was the Lord's original intention that every person born into the world would be an automatic member of His assembly. However, the advent of sin resulted in the creation of an alternate assembly populated by those who would rather associate with God's nemesis, Satan. The dividing line between the two assemblies is God's holy law of love. Those who align their wills with the Lord choose to observe it in totality, while those associated with Satan either reject it completely or obey only those sections they deem convenient.

Affiliation with the evil assembly is not simply determined by intermittent violations of God's law. The people who feel at home in it have made a conscious decision to be there. Interested only in their own pleasure, they consistently reject the pleadings of the Holy Spirit. They have even gotten to a place in their life where they feel no remorse for their evil. The fact that guilt filled Adam and Eve after they transgressed God's explicit command evidences their sorrow for breaking relationship with their Creator. Adversely, the story of Cain is one of an individual who made a conscious choice to live in opposition to his Maker.

Judging from the biblical account, Cain was definitely a religious person. He was just as committed to the ritualistic acts of presenting an offering to the Lord as was his brother, Abel (Gen. 4:3, 4). However, his outward conformity had no inward sincerity. As a result, his rebellious spirit nullified the validity of his offering. God's concern for Cain led Him to make a personal intervention, which has many lessons for *us*. The very fact that He noticed Cain's internal conflict lets us know that He does not give up on us at the first sign of rebellion (verse 6). He wanted to have a relationship with him, but knew that as long as Cain allowed himself to be controlled by depression and anger he would never be open to the leading of the Holy Spirit.

Hence, in an effort to steer him to the right path, God reminded the young rebel, "If you do well, will you not be accepted?" (verse 7). God's very question implies a code of behavior to which He expected Cain to abide. Undoubtedly, adherence to the law demanded discipline, but the alternative was dire: "If you do not do well, sin is lurking at the door; its desire is for you, but you must master it" (verse 7). Unfortunately, sin eventually walked through Cain's door and possessed him so fully that he committed fratricide (verses 8-10).

Cain's recalcitrance serves as an archetypical profile of those who choose to leave the circle of safety. God's covenant space contains love, peace, joy, patience, and the entire roster of virtues that add value to living. Once a person leaves this zone, all that remains is sadness, disaster, and the illusion of happiness enabled by money, mind-altering substances, and possessions. After years of watching revered celebrities exhibit their unhappiness on the international public stage, I find it hard to comprehend why so many still succumb to Satan's lies and seek happiness in the hedonistic excess promoted by the entertainment industry. Yet, just as He did with Cain, the Spirit of God never ceases to plead with sinners to return to His covenant family.

Adam and Eve must have carried immense guilt for the turmoil in their home. Although they had repented of their sins, nothing could reverse the results. Concerned about the future of creation, they must have breathed a sigh of relief when it appeared as if Seth's progeny would maintain the holy standard that Cain's descendants appeared to despise. In fact, it was during the days of Seth's son, Enosh, that there appeared to be a revival among the sparse populace (verse 26). Unfortunately, the Bible informs us that generations later the picture was rather bleak, and wickedness had consumed the world's inhabitants. It was so bad that God Himself debated whether to destroy His creation (Gen. 6:1-8). However, although terribly diminished, His church was not totally decimated and a faithful remnant guaranteed creation's preservation.

Noah's favor with God stemmed from the fact that he deliberately remained loyal to the terms of the covenant. The Bible boasts that he was a "righteous man, blameless in his generation" (verse 9). Obviously he knew that holy living was a choice. It would have been easy for him to go along with the majority, but he realized that he could find true security only in the arms of his Maker. Indeed, his designation as a "righteous" and "blameless" person has a distinct context. The fact that he needed grace suggests that he was not blameless in the "never done anything wrong" sense (verse 8). It was his blessed Redeemer who had bestowed the righteousness and perfection upon him.

Almost as if it is warning us about the danger of falling into the pit of self-righteous legalism, the biblical record reminds us that even the blameless Noah had moments of weakness. Not long after the divinely dramatic rescue from the cataclysmic Flood, this same "righteous" stalwart experimented with alcohol and got so "stoned" that he passed out. Ironically, it was on the lips of a barely sober man that God placed a prophecy that would launch the next phase of His church (Gen. 9:24-27). Indeed, it was in fulfillment of this prophecy that the obedient Abraham left the relative luxury of Haran to seek God's will in the Hamitic territory of Canaan.

From the Promise to the River

We can never be certain about the moral impact of Noah's drunkenness on his sons and grandsons, but it is clear that the inhabitants of the earth had already started slipping away from God just several generations after the Flood. The decision to build a fortified skyscraper not only proved their disbelief in God's covenant promise never again to destroy the world by a flood, but also indicated their desire to outsmart Him. Beguiled by their own ingenuity, they actually thought that human wisdom could avert the judgments of God. It was this blatant act of rebellion that led to the division of the world among the various linguistic groups. However, even with the geographical separation, God did not leave Himself without a witness, and remnants of His law of love survived across the globe.

According to Muslim tradition, Abraham's resistance to his tribe's idolatrous habits placed him in the divine spotlight.[1] Although the Bible does not corroborate such a version of events, we do see a picture of a man of faith who is willing to act on the sole authority of God's Word. Not only did he leave his ancestral home to live in a distant territory, but he was even willing to sever his son's jugular vein if that's what godly obedience demanded. That is not to say that he was a perfect man. When circumstances had him cornered and the man of faith feared for his life, he surrendered principle for deception as he lied about his relationship with Sarah. His willingness to save his own skin by sacrificing his wife's virtue was not just a one-time thing. According to his own testimony, when exposed the second time it was a preplanned strategy (Gen. 20:13). Nonetheless, it was with this man of fragile faith that God entrusted the responsibility of being His representative on earth.

Although Abraham was God's visible agent, he was not the only one to whom the Lord had revealed His will. In fact, it appears as if God placed others in his path to guide him in the right direction. For instance, when he lied to the Egyptian pharaoh and the Gerarite Abimelech about his marriage status, it was they who instructed him on the sinfulness of adultery (Gen. 12:18, 19; 20:10).[2] Recognizing that he was not the only one with a godly understanding of right and wrong, Abraham explained to Abimelech, "I did it because I thought, 'There is no fear of God at all in this place, and they will kill me because of my wife'" (Gen. 20:11). Little did he know that the God of grace had revealed His moral statutes to all people. Abraham's elevated role in the scheme of things was to preserve an *accurate* account of those statutes through his physical and spiritual descendants.

Several hundred years after Abraham's death God would establish a system that codified the behavioral criteria for kingdom citizens. As we have discussed extensively in previous chapters, the revealed law was not an explanation of what they needed to do to access the kingdom, but was a description of a kingdom dweller's profile. In other words, citizenship preceded responsibility. The Israelites whom God had called were far from perfect and many were ignorant of the law's statutes, yet the Lord chose them to represent Him. By adhering closely to His precepts, they were the ones who would model His love to the world. Surrounding nations would find themselves attracted to a people who loved their spouses, cared for the poor and needy, and enjoyed God's company so much that they refrained from business one day a week to bask in His presence. Ellen G. White reminds us, "If we would humble ourselves before God, and be kind and courteous and tenderhearted and pitiful, there would be one hundred conversions to the truth where now there is only one."[3]

Sadly, Israel's history was less than exemplary, and rather than influence society for good, society swayed God's chosen. When we reflect on Israel's plight, it would not be unfair to ask whether the omniscient God made a mistake. After all, why would He select a people who He knew would fail their commission? While such a question has a logical basis, we must not forget that God's foreknowledge does not mean that everything will work out according to His plan. Other forces are at work, the most powerful of which is human free will. He knows what choices we *will* make, because those are precisely the choices that we *did* make. What kind of God would He be if He knew we were going to sin but allowed the temptation anyhow? The kingdom consists of volunteers who choose to align their lives to His loving principles. He offers incentives to those who choose to abide in Him and warns of the dangers for those who stray, but He never forces people to make a decision against their will.

Given Israel's tragic failure, it would not be wrong to say that Satan experienced significant success in his attempt to disqualify the people whom God had selected. The incipient wickedness that permeated both kingdoms of Israel and Judah was definitely not a testimony of righteousness. Because of the people's blatant disregard for God's law of love, in no way could they claim to be the hub of God's visible kingdom. Nonetheless, even in Israel's most calamitous hour there were stalwarts who valiantly sounded the call to kingdom principles as they cried out against economic injustice, political corruption, religious hypocrisy, moral depravity, and other sinful actions at odds with God's loving law. Indeed, many generations later when the remnant of Israel found themselves subject to the yoke of Rome, one of those voices would announce the final phase of God's assembly.

From the River to the Remnant

John the Baptist established his open-air meeting place on the very banks of the Jordan River where his ancestors had seen God work in mighty ways. His teachings contained the same principles of social justice heralded by his forebears: Isaiah, Hosea, Amos, and Micah. He understood that fidelity to God's law manifest itself in acts of charity and integrity (see Luke 3:10-14). Too often, those who claim to follow Christ speak of their spiritual life in negative terms. When asked to explain their faith, they are quick to say what they *don't* do. By the time they have provided an extended list of prohibited foods, pastimes, and Sabbath activities, the inquirer wonders, "What *do* you do?"

John's preaching was a sober reminder that God's assembly should not be known for its inactivity, but for its loving involvement in the affairs of the Creator and His creation. Notice that he did not burden his baptismal candidates with a list of liturgical requirements. Undoubtedly he knew that the church was a worshipping community, but he had seen the hypocrisy in those who were overly concerned about the intricacies of Sabbathkeeping, but had no regard for the "least of these" in their environs. John reminded his listeners that God's people are not selective in their law observance, but understand that the law seeks to help create loving communities based on inclusive acts of service rather than exclusive worship rituals.

With his clear call to loving reform and justice, John truly prepared the way for Jesus. Their methods were definitely different, but their message was the same. Like His earthly cousin, the one who is Immanuel reminded those who claim to walk with God that the church is an assembly of people who are on a mission to vindicate His Father's tarnished name before a watching universe (Matt. 5:14-16). It is not selfish individuals on an esoteric quest for sinless perfection who will achieve the vindication of God's name. Our Father's name is exonerated when His children understand that true love for Him means placing His priorities before ours. God's called-out people will demonstrate that it is possible for human beings to be so filled with the Spirit that their actions embody the essence of the kingdom to which they pledge primary allegiance (see Rom. 12:9-21). After all, when the time comes for Him to gather the faithful, it is only those personifying His law of love who will hear the blessed "well done" from His lips (Matt. 25:31-46).

True members of God's faithful assembly recognize that their affiliation is not forced or inherited, but voluntary. Each person must make a personal decision to be not "conformed to this world, but be transformed by the renewing of [their] minds, so that [they] may discern what is the will of God—what is good and acceptable and perfect" (Rom. 12:2). Kingdom citizens have always been aware that God reveals His will through His law. It drives them to yield to its precepts, even when warring internal passions make submission difficult (1 Peter 2:11). They fight their natural sinful inclination, not to gain God's favor, but because they already realize that they are recipients of His grace. It is the hope in them that drives them to represent the holiness of God through a loving commitment to His charitable law (Col. 1:27).

Unfortunately, the central role of God's law has faded during the centuries of the development of the religion that we now call Christianity. As the successive generations of Jesus' followers became more institutionalized, philosophically generated creeds usurped the place of God's law of liberty. While many of the new doctrines and regulations came from good intentions, they quickly replaced Jesus' dynamic legacy of love with a staid roster of intellectual propositions. An *assembly* that should have been known for its commitment to living out the principles of God's love mutated into a *society* concerned only with the transmission of tradition. Even more troubling is the reality that a *body* commissioned to perform the works of the Spirit has morphed into an *institution* corrupted by power-hungry politicians.

As my dear friend and mentor Charles E. Bradford recognizes, it's time for us to revisit the "body" metaphor through the discipline of *physiology* rather than *anatomy*. In other words, the people of God must stop simply *talking* about what constitutes the church, and start *being* the church. In His final earthly message to His inner circle, Jesus already informed us how we can know that we are *being* what His Father has called us to be (John 13:35). Unfortunately, a brief survey of the history of the Jesus movement yields a shocking account of people who have strayed from the ideal. Instead of emulating His compassionated ministry, they commandeered the Savior's name to serve their own imperial quests.[4] Under the alleged banner of the Prince of Peace, they have tried, executed, or enslaved countless numbers. The underhanded actions of such Christian institutions have placed them among the earthly governments that God will destroy when He finally announces the Messiah's kingdom (Rev. 11:15).

It is in the midst of such cacophonous apostasy that God has called a remnant to reflect His genuine will to a world confused by the hypocrisy of nominal Christians and the ecclesial institutions to which they belong. This remnant comprises those who truly know what it means to "keep the commandments of God and hold the testimony of Jesus" (Rev. 12:17). While they remind professed followers of Christ that all of God's commandments are binding on the faithful, they don't elevate the fourth so highly that they forget about the others. Numbered among the remnant are people who understand that God's Spirit must so possess His church that everything taking place in it will bring glory to His name.

Conclusion

Satan has steadily worked to discredit the church of God before the world. By introducing the notion of "Christendom," he has given the impression that the institution that claims to represent Christ on earth is itself a temporal power that operates under the same rules as other earthly governments. The stratified distinction between "clergy" and "laity" has served as a cover for all manner of institutional abuse, as those in positions of "authority" find new ways to manipulate the gullible masses. Those claiming to speak for God have disrespected His law and introduced false doctrines into the Christian mainstream. We are currently in an age of Christian confusion, in which two extremes serve the devil's purpose. On one hand are those "conservative" churches that are so arrogant that they refuse to admit their illogical rejection of the Ten Commandments they claim to uphold. The other pole includes the liberals, who shamelessly promote a Woodstock agenda that heralds the death of moral guidelines.

Although it is those two extremes that most often get media attention, God knows who His real people are. His assembly may not have popular name recognition, but its members have remained true to the call He has placed upon them. In the midst of apostasy they cherish truth and hold fast to the legacy of righteousness that has been theirs even before sin entered human reality. Expedience or compromise does not determine their mission, but they listen only to the instructions that emanate from the lips of our loving Lord. In reflecting on the special nature of the church throughout time, Ellen G. White writes: "During ages of spiritual darkness the church of God has been as a city set on a hill. From age to age, through successive generations, the pure doctrines of heaven have been unfolding within its borders. Enfeebled and defective as it may appear, the church is the one object upon which God bestows in a special sense His supreme regard. It is the theater of His grace, in which He delights to reveal His power to transform hearts."[5]

Recently I had a conversation with a sincere believer who spoke about the necessity of calling for uniformity in the Adventist "brand." A fairly recent convert, she felt that the witness of the church was being hurt, because everyone had not embraced a nineteenth-century-style dress reform, and that there are some in our ranks who still eat flesh. If only everyone could get on the same page, she reasoned, the church would attract millions. I affirmed her zeal for reformation, but cautioned her about focusing on quantifiable externals. Appealing for the Spirit's intervention, I then said: "The only brand that really matters in God's kingdom is *love*—a love that manifests itself in our relationships with Him and our fellow human beings." She paused for a moment before remarking, "That makes sense. This will be my message from now on." As you reflect on the important role of God's law in identifying the people of God, will it also be yours?

[1] Koran, 21 (Al-'Anbiya').

[2] See discussion in K. A. Burton, *The Blessing of Africa*, pp. 74, 75, 93-95. Coincidentally, the lesson not only highlighted the seriousness of adultery, but challenged him to demonstrate his love for his wife.

[3] Ellen G. White, *Testimonies for the Church* (Mountain View, Calif.: Pacific Press Pub. Assn., 1948), vol. 9, p. 189.

[4] For a discussion on the way in which some have used Christianity for imperialistic aims, see Burton, *Blessing of Africa*, pp. 173-206.

[5] Ellen G. White, *The Acts of the Apostles* (Mountain View, Calif.: Pacific Press Pub. Assn., 1911), p. 12.

CHAPTER 13

Christ's Kingdom and the Law

I'm not sure when my interest in genealogy started. Though I have always been excited about meeting new relatives, at a certain time in my life I felt compelled to find out *how* we were related. It is possible that Martha Matilda Josephs, my maternal grandmother, planted the seed in me. I still recall the summer of 1986 when from her wheelchair she informed me that we were related to the Jamaican prime ministers Norman and Michael Manley. Because my genealogical interest was only tepid at the time, I didn't make the effort to record her detailed explanation of the names and relationships of the people that made us family.

On second thought, my curiosity in discovering my family's roots could have come from my mother. When I was still in short pants, I remember asking her why she signed her name "Cynthia Morgan-Burton." The hyphenated signature was confusing to a lad who bore only the last of the two surnames. Mummy shared with me that it had been passed on to her that we were direct descendants of Captain Henry Morgan, the pirate-turned-politician who served as a lieutenant governor of Jamaica.

Whatever the source of my genealogical fascination, whenever I get some spare time I like to find ways to connect the dots. On my maternal side I've managed to recover details that go back four generations to my great-great-grandparents, Alexander Josephs and Lavina Thompson. On my father's side I've been able to retrieve information for only my great-grandparents, Charles Burton and Cecelia Johnson (I also learned that my grandfather's middle name was not "Augustus," as my father thought, but "Elnezar"). For the most part, however, the research is very difficult. I have yet to find living relatives who can further verify the Manley and Morgan links, and the sociohistorical reality of slavery's legacy means that my quest to determine my complicated past may be an unreachable dream.

Most recently I delved deeper into my research by ordering a DNA test, chiefly to determine my African roots. My blood does consist of contributions from Caucasian and Jewish ancestors, but it is my African forebears that have given most to my external identity. Neglecting to assess the complexity of slavery, I underwent the test with the naive expectation that I would know for sure from which African *tribe* my relatives hailed. The results left me with more questions than answers. I discovered that my African ancestors hailed from geographically diverse regions identified today as Cape Verde, Guinea-Bissau, Angola, Mozambique, Rwanda, and Morocco. At the time of writing, I have been in possession of this knowledge for less than a month, and still can't figure out if I'm underwhelmed by the disappointment of not being able to pinpoint a single ancestral location, or overwhelmed by the research that lies ahead as I try to determine which generation came from where.

My wife, pretty much content being acquainted with only the relatives that she currently knows, recently inquired about my fascination (she may have used the term *obsession*, but that's just semantics!). She couldn't understand why I would invest in a test that told me what I already knew (that I had African ancestors). I shared with her my frustration at being in conversations in which others could confidently talk about their Irish, Scottish, Italian, or German ancestry, but I was totally oblivious to the sections of the African continent from which my people hailed. I wanted an anchor point—somewhere to call "home."

Home is such a tenuous term. I currently reside in Harvest, Alabama, where I have set up "home" with my nuclear family. However, after living in the United States for almost 30 years, I still carry the status of "resident alien." I pay my taxes, qualify for government benefits, and am subject to the laws, but I am still a foreigner. Even after I receive citizenship, I will still bear the stigma of being "naturalized," as if there were a time that I was unnatural. Since I am not fully embraced by my adopted nation, one could conclude that I can find a "home" in the land of my birth. Nevertheless, as a child of colonial immigrants, I can never claim (although I was born in England) to be "English," but must bear the imperial designation "British subject."

At times I just claim Jamaica as my home. After all, it is the nationality of my mother and Cuban-born father. However, whenever I visit that beautiful island, I have to stand in the long visitors' line at passport control as *real* Jamaican nationals breeze through their designated lane. Recently I learned that I could qualify for citizenship through my parents, but would it really make the country "home"? Further, although several generations of my family have lived in Jamaica, the African ones were abducted from their real home. I guess I could choose one of the countries from my complex genealogy, but what would be the basis for the choice? Plus, although I have proof of ancestral belongings, entry to any one of those countries would still require a visa.

With so many places to call "home" I still have a sense of homelessness. Earth has no place to which I can pledge full allegiance. My loyalties find themselves conflicted during sporting events and international incidents. I feel personally vested in the political process and quality of life in all of those places. The only thing that brings me sanity is the recognition that all of my earthly geopolitical markers are temporary dwelling places soon to be consumed by Christ's eternal kingdom. Indeed, it is His kingdom and the principles that govern it that will be the central theme in this final chapter.

Axis of Evil

The Genesis account of creation tells of a God who created our world with the intention that it would always be His kingdom. He entrusted "dominion" as a type of proxy monarch to Adam, but the fact that he was a created being is evidence enough that he was subordinate to his Creator. Had Adam not sinned, his governance configuration would have been an eternal reality. However, his attempt to usurp godly prerogatives thwarted the original plan in which righteous principles would rule for eternity. Instead, the creation upon which God had pronounced His endorsement was now occupied by an antithetical force on a mission of destruction.

Adam probably never thought about the ramifications of his apostasy. In effect, when he disobeyed God the scepter entrusted to him went to another. It is in this context that we understand how Satan could appear in the divine council as earth's representative (Job 1:6). The master of deception knew exactly what he was doing when he tricked the first couple. Following Adam's sin, he could rightly claim to be the "god of this world" and the "prince of the power of the air" (2 Cor. 4:4; Eph. 2:2, NIV). When he offered Jesus ownership over all of earth's governments, he was operating well within his rights (Matt. 4:8, 9). He had deceived Adam into giving him the title deed, knowing that with the transfer Adam's status would change. Now, rather than exercising dominion, Adam would be under dominion. To add insult to injury, not only was he subject to Satan's repressive rule, but he would be at enmity with some of the very animals over which he had once had control.

Satan annexed the world with the sole intention of distorting everything that God had declared good. Nothing was out-of-bounds. The Lord had created healthy humans and animals. Lion and lamb frolicked side by side in the open meadows. The weather system ensured a plentiful yield of nutritious crops to satisfy the huge demand for nourishment. Human hearts were attuned to the happiness of one another. But Satan would change all this. Viruses, bad vision, bone fractures, and other ailments would attack human health. The egalitarian coexistence among animals would give way to a system of predators versus prey. Droughts, floods, tornadoes, and other crop-destroying weather systems would hijack the world's temperature-controlled atmosphere. Additionally, the stench of selfishness and the canker of competition would overwhelm the fragrance of love that the Father had infused in the heart of His children.

While it may seem as if the architect of destruction is disorganized and impulsive in the way he manages the earth, we shouldn't underestimate him. He was a highly exalted angel with superior intelligence and has calculated his every move. Is it a coincidence that insurance companies refer to destructive weather systems as "acts of God"? Why is it that professed Christians could believe that God engineered a massacre of infants because He wanted more angels in heaven?[1] And why do secular psychologists and liberal theologians appease those who are confused about their sexual identity with the explanation that it is the way God *made* them? Such concepts come not from an immature opponent, but from one who is so sophisticated that he has successfully distorted the image of God in the minds of many. Always on the trail of deception, Satan has people believing that God is the cause of maladies that he himself has orchestrated.

His strategy is nothing short of genius. On the one hand, it has people paying homage to Satan while thinking they are honoring the Lord. On the other hand, it has people so upset with God for damaging their home or killing their children that they want nothing to do with Him. Upon further reflection, his strategy impacts a third category of people: the ones who are aware of the true source of evil, but are quick to relegate the unconsciously deceived into the camp of the damned. They are also affected by the devil's strategy, because like the other two categories, they fail to comprehend the God of grace who grants a waiver for people's ignorance (Acts 17:30). Though Satan may be a genius, he can never outsmart the God who examines every intention before making a final judgment on an individual's eternal destiny.

The enemies of God's kingdom are not the people who are naive in their positions, but the ones who knowingly take a stand with Satan. With unapologetic defiance, they shun the principles of God's loving law and promote a hedonistic agenda that glorifies everything evil. Nowhere is this more prominent in our age than in the entertainment industry. Popular entertainers have become digital gods who double as evangelists of evil. Rare is the celebrity immunized from the raucous recklessness of rude behavior. Addictions, profanity, adultery, and homosexuality appear to be their norm, and they are unrestrained in their promotion of their decadent lifestyle to the masses whose filthy lucre has enabled their deification.

I still remember George W. Bush's State of the Union address in 2002 when he introduced the world to the phrase "axis of evil." In his mind, America and the "coalition of the willing" constituted agents of righteousness divinely appointed to quash terrorism and governments hostile to free-market capitalism. The second time I recall him using the phrase was about a month later when he used binoculars to peer into North Korea from South Korea. While I concur with President Bush about the obvious evil behind a tyrannous system that oppresses its populace, I believe his understanding of the "axis of evil" needs some spiritual adjustment. He could very well have replaced the binoculars with a powerful satellite that has the ability of scoping the entire globe. In reality, the entire world is a part of the axis of evil. No nation is immune.

Resident Aliens

The fact that the world is currently under Satan's governance has serious implications for the follower of Christ. Of necessity, we must live in the world, but do we really belong here? On one level, we could answer in the affirmative. Indeed, we are citizens of nations, and several places in the Bible encourage us to cooperate with the political process. Peter urges his audience to "accept the authority of every human institution, whether of the emperor as supreme, or of governors, as sent by him to punish those who do wrong and to praise those who do right" (1 Peter 2:13, 14). Paul uses more direct language when he writes, "Let every person be subject to the governing authorities; for there is no authority except from God, and those authorities that exist have been instituted by God" (Rom. 13:1). Jesus Himself commanded His followers to "render to Caesar the things that are Caesar's" (Mark 12:17, KJV).

In no uncertain terms such texts encourage the fledgling Jesus movement to cooperate with the political status quo. However, it would be a mistake to read them as calls to mindless nationalism. Unfortunately, too many Christians apply those texts in isolation and have developed an unhealthy love affair with their tribes and lands of their birth. In the buildup to World War II the Seventh-day Adventist Church in Germany was so enamored with Adolf Hitler's reformist policies that the leadership failed to serve as the prophetic voice for their Jewish siblings who were in desperate need for vocal Christian allies.[2] More recently a prominent Seventh-day Adventist Church leader was convicted for his role in the Hutu slaughter of Tutsis during the horrific Rwandan genocide.[3] While such cases may seem extreme, the potential for similar things to happen in any number of places in the Seventh-day Adventist world is very real. Whenever symbols of a nation get woven into religious culture and church members uncritically support government policies, there exists a breeding ground for the enemy of souls to recruit soldiers for his divisive cause.

Before interpreting the passages as blanket calls to pledge allegiance to earthly states, it behooves us to revisit their contexts. Remember, the biblical writers made such exhortations at a time when the imperial Roman government ruled with an iron fist and did not harbor favorable feelings toward Judaism and its messianic offspring. In no way would Christ or any of His spokespersons encourage believers to cast their lot with such an oppressive political machine. Their appeals were not calls to compromise, but were motivated by divine wisdom. By cooperating with the state on issues that enhance community, believers have broader opportunities to share their faith (1 Peter 2:15; Rom. 13:8-10).

While upholding societal laws, believers must focus on their primary allegiance. Although they may possess a birth certificate and a passport that identify their place of birth and domicile, they remember that their true citizenship is with the kingdom of God. Consequently, inasmuch as they may be involved in the affairs of society, they never forget their true status in this world. They may rise to top administrative levels in government and industry, but—like every other Christian—their position there has been afforded for the purpose of witness. Of necessity they must be *in* the world, but they are not *of* the world (Rom. 12:2). Through their principled actions they continually remind their colleagues that their "citizenship is in heaven" (Phil. 3:20).

Children of God must never forget their true status in this age. Especially in nations experiencing relative peace and prosperity, it is easy to get lulled to complacency by the promise of government entitlements and the easy access to food, comfort, and entertainment. However, in spite of how delightful life may be for some of us at the present, we must not forget that we don't belong here. Peter refers to us as "aliens and exiles" (1 Peter 2:11). As aliens, we recognize our status as strangers in a foreign territory in which the culture of the host nation is at odds with that of God's kingdom. Although we want so much to do our part in society, we must not blend in to the point that we forget our true roots. We must always remember the fact that in addition to being aliens, we are also exiles. The exilic qualifier to our alien status is a calm reminder that our situation is transitory. Not permanent residents, we are temporary sojourners who expect to return home one day.

Since we are just passing through, we refuse to embrace the values of worldly governments. We know who we are: ambassadors of the eternal kingdom who represent the Almighty. It is with this recognition that Peter urges the "aliens and exiles to abstain from the desires of the flesh that wage war against the soul" (verse 11). Despite living in a culture of profligate lawlessness, we hold firm to the loving principles embedded in God's unchangeable law. In a sense, we are a part of a resistance movement that will not be "conformed to the world, but will be transformed by a daily renewal of our mind" (see Rom. 12:2). As citizens of Augustine's city of God who participate in affairs of the state, we refuse to align ourselves to the city of the world.

New World Order

Kingdom citizens endure the challenges of living in the world's city by holding on to the hope that the Messiah will soon reclaim Adam's legacy for humanity. In fact, it is the hope that infuses meaning into our continued fidelity to God. It reminds us that the plan of salvation is more than an esoteric doctrine. The Lord doesn't just save us from our sins for the sake of it, but for a purpose. God desires unrestricted communion with us, but that will not happen until the barriers of evil are permanently annihilated. Until then, the believer's relationship with God is impeded by the sinful reality of our existence (1 Cor. 13:12). Thankfully, such a dilemma is not the believer's eternal fate. At this very moment God is making preparations for an indestructible future in which He will never again be estranged from His creation (John 14:1-3).

Given the fact that our current dilemma resulted from the sin of two perfectly created humans, some may wonder how I can speak so confidently about an eternity without sin. After all, if evil forced its way into our reality once, why can't it do it again? It is a fair question, and I won't even pretend to have a comprehensive answer. However, I can find comfort in the promises of God's Word. Daniel sees a time that "the sovereignty, power and greatness of all the kingdoms under heaven will be handed over to the holy people of the Most High. His kingdom will be an *everlasting* kingdom, and all rulers will worship and obey him" (Dan. 7:27, NIV). John echoes the same promise when he announces the moment when "the kingdom of the world has become the kingdom of our Lord and of his Messiah, and he will reign *for ever and ever*" (Rev. 11:15, NIV). In no uncertain terms, the Bible declares that the final world power will be principled, unrivaled, and *eternal*. God's kingdom will have no end. When George Frideric Handel meditated on this reality, it evoked so much emotion that he felt compelled to compose the "Hallelujah Chorus."

Our finite minds cannot fully comprehend the radically transformative nature of God's eternal kingdom. In our current age political states are complex machines with seemingly endless bureaucratic levels, amendable constitutions, and questionable legal systems. However, in the age to come, the entire government will be upon the shoulders of "the Mighty God, the Everlasting Father, the Prince of Peace." It will have no need for elected lawmakers, because each person would automatically know what was required of them. Jeremiah provides a preview of such an age: "'This is the covenant I will make with the people of Israel after that time,' declares the Lord. 'I will put my law in their minds and write it on their hearts. I will be their God, and they will be my people. No longer will they teach their neighbor, or say to one another, "*Know the Lord*," because they will all know me, from the least of them to the greatest,' declares the Lord" (Jer. 31:33, 34, NIV).

This is a liberating thought. With the eradication of sin, believers will no longer experience conflict in their relationship with God. Currently, our efforts to follow His revealed guidelines constantly struggle with selfish desires, which the devil uses to his advantage. However, when evil and all of its dimensions are permanently erased from our reality, submitting to the principles of His loving law will be the natural thing to do! The death of sin also means the end of all the bad things that it introduced to the world. "Discomfort," "disease," "disorder," "despair," "dismay," and "disappointment" will no longer have an entry in the dictionary. Looking forward to that glorious day, the prophet of Patmos writes, "He will wipe every tear from their eyes. There will be no more death or mourning or crying or pain, for the old order of things has passed away" (Rev. 21:4, NIV).

The new world order that comes about with the restoration of heaven and earth is really a delightful return to the original world order. Isaiah illustrates life under the eternal kingdom with words that evoke nostalgic expectation: "The wolf will live with the lamb, the leopard will lie down with the goat, the calf and the lion and the yearling together; and a little child will lead them. The cow will feed with the bear, their young will lie down together, and the lion will eat straw like the ox. The infant will play near the cobra's den, the young child will put its hand into the viper's nest. They will neither harm nor destroy on all my holy mountain, for the earth will be filled with the knowledge of the Lord as the waters cover the sea" (Isa. 11:6-9, NIV). Such an un-Darwinian picture of harmonious cooperation between the species is a gentle reminder that God's law of love will be imprinted on every heart—both human and animal.

Loving fellowship will not be limited to only humans and animals, but in the same fashion as our primal ancestors, we will also have an opportunity for unmediated communion with our Maker. Speaking through Isaiah, the Lord Himself informs us of our regular appointments in the renewed earth: "From new moon to new moon, and from sabbath to sabbath, all flesh shall come to worship before me" (Isa. 66:23). Believers are even now rehearsing for kingdom life. By abiding by the eternal principles of God's holy law, they are afforded a taste of eternity when righteousness will rule every heart. In anticipation of spending eternity with their Maker, they choose fidelity over adultery, respect over rudeness, charity over greed, peace over war, truth over falsehood, Sabbath over Sunday, and truth over error. They don't do this *to* gain access to the kingdom, but they honor their Redeemer because they *have it already.*

Conclusion

Until God fully reveals the kingdom, believers must endure a paradoxical existence. We live in an age in which the forces of evil have launched a multifaceted attack against God's kingdom. In some instances those assaults are blatantly evil as despots and sadists kill, pillage, and oppress with impunity. On other occasions, the incursions are subtly launched as Satan attempts to pacify our spiritual awareness with comfortable lives and questionable entertainment. Those of us enjoying the "benefits" of a capitalist society should be especially mindful of Satan's strategy, particularly as we witness the gradual disappearance of the moral line between church and state. Only those who remain alert and vigilant will do what it takes to maintain commitment to the Master in this axis of evil.

While participating in world affairs, believers know that no nation can ever receive their full allegiance. Like the four highly placed refugee-turned-politicians in Daniel's book, their first loyalty is to God's kingdom. They remain true to those principles even if it means getting thrown into blazing furnaces or lions' dens. Such resident aliens also match their love for God with their love for fellow human beings. As people who understand the true principle behind God's holy law of love, they find opportunities to alleviate poverty, empower the oppressed, and give a voice to the voiceless. They do all this because they won't be comfortable until "justice [rolls] down like waters, and righteousness like an ever-flowing stream" (Amos 5:24). Not until Christ makes "all things new" (Rev. 21:5) will they feel at peace.

At the time of renewal, God will restore the earth to its pristine beauty, and innocence will reign once more. Those who carried the stigma of alien residency in the world's kingdom will be elevated to the status of full citizens with all the rights and privileges that come with that designation. Citizenship in the new kingdom does not derive from one's place of birth or parental pedigree, but through the acceptance of the salvation that is ours through the blood of Christ. All who truly accept Christ's atoning sacrifice choose to enter into a covenant relationship with Him. They express their loyalty by ordering their life according to the principles of the kingdom that God has revealed in His loving law—it's as if they are speaking the language of a new nation even before they emigrate to its shores. On that day when the Lord fully inaugurates the kingdom, He Himself will implant His righteousness into their very DNA as they "dwell in the kingdom of God for evermore" (see Ps. 23:6).

---

[1] In a service commemorating those massacred at the Sandy Hook Elementary School in Connecticut, a pastor, Robert Weiss, reportedly said of one of the victims, "She was supposed to be an angel in the play; now she's an angel up in heaven." See Ernest Scheyder and Rob Cox, "Children in Connecticut Rampage, All 6 and 7, Shot Repeatedly," *Reuters,* Dec, 15, 2012, www.reuters.com/article/2012/12/15/us-connecticut-towns-idUSBRE8BD0U120121215.

[2] For a concise summary, see Corrie Schroder, "Seventh Day Adventists," www.history.ucsb.edu/projects/holocaust/Research/Proseminar/corrieschroder.htm.

[3] See BBC News article, "Pastor Aided Rwanda Genocide," http://news.bbc.co.uk/2/hi/africa/2778839.stm. There is also a best-selling book named after a letter Tutsi members wrote to the convicted pastor: Philip Gourevitch, *We Wish to Inform You That Tomorrow We Will be Killed With Our Families: Stories From Rwanda* (New York: Picador, 1999).

Epilogue

On that calamitous prayer meeting night when I received a speeding citation, the police officer presented me with two options. I could either pay the fine through the mail, or I could take my chances in front of a judge. If I took the first option, in addition to admitting guilt, it would add penalty points to my driver's license. However, if I chose to go to court, I would still have to pay a fine, but I would also have the opportunity to attend traffic school. While I would have to pay extra for the class, my driver's license would stay clean.

Although it prolonged the overall process, I chose the second option. Points on my license could mean an increase in insurance costs, so I would end up paying one way or the other. Traffic school was actually very informative. After we watched gory video footage of motor vehicle accidents, the instructor presented us with practical tips on defensive driving and speed prevention. The four hours flew by faster than I had anticipated. When I left the police station, I was careful to apply every strategy the officer shared with us. Determined never to get another ticket, I pledged to myself that I would never speed again!

The Sunday after traffic school I was scheduled to attend an important service at the church. A preteen had been diagnosed with a rare illness, and we were going to have a special prayer session for her. With the driving instruction still fresh in my mind, I made it a point to leave my home 30 minutes earlier than normal. I was not going to put myself in a position in which I would have to speed to make it to church on time. As the time for departure drew closer, I realized that I would not have time to eat a decent breakfast, so I made a quick sandwich and put some fruit in a brown bag so that I could eat on the way. The sandwich was so good and the road so clear that I did not even realize that I was driving highway speed on a country lane. I think you know the rest of the story. Fortunately, I received a second chance to go to traffic school (this time for two sessions), but it definitely hurt to pay another whopping fine.

As I reflect on my experience, I can't help praising God. Don't get me wrong. I'm not at all thankful for the tickets, but I am glad that God does not deal with us in the merciless manner of the court. The truth is, we are all guilty of speeding down life's highway—we have all transgressed God's holy law. However, when we become aware of our sin, God doesn't immediately burden us with the law's penalty, but offers us His grace. He knows that every sinner did not set out deliberately to commit sin, and many do not realize their transgression until after the fact. The Lord also knows that some who may have consciously sinned are plagued with guilt and desperately desire relief. Sensitive to our needs, He is always ready to release us from the penalty for our sins.

God's forgiveness is a gift to us, but it came at great expense to Him. The law we transgressed He established for the sake of harmony and order, and He can't just look the other way when we cause conflict and upheaval. What we do affects things. It is for that very reason that the divine Christ entered our reality. He came as our representative to bear the penalty for our sins. The consequences that should be ours have been transferred to Him.

Christ's sacrifice for us in no way weakens the importance of the law. If anything, it demonstrates its significance. As a result, those who have benefited from God's grace are expected to order their life according to His law. They appreciate the fact that its principles seek to encourage loving relationships that pull us closer to one another and to our Creator. The redeemed keep God's law because they understand that it is the immutable constitution for the eternal kingdom, and those who have chosen to side with God will want to live according to His will. As others succumb to satanic pressure and turn to hybrid religious systems, the grateful recipients of grace respond to John's call for endurance as they "keep the commandments of God and hold fast to the faith of Jesus" (Rev. 14:12).